FEED ALL MY SHEEP

FEED ALL MY SHEEP

A Guide and Curriculum for Adults
with Developmental Disabilities

Doris C. Clark
with music by Kinley Lange

Geneva Press
Louisville, Kentucky

Scripture quotations are taken from the *New American Standard Bible,* © 1960, 1962, 1963, 1968, 1971, 1972, 1973, 1975, 1977 by The Lockman Foundation. Used by permission. Scripture quotations marked NIV are from *The Holy Bible, New International Version.* Copyright ©1973, 1978, 1984 International Bible Society. Used by permission of Zondervan Bible Publishers.

Book design by Anthony Liptak
Cover design and illustration by Rohani Design

First edition
Published by Geneva Press
Louisville, Kentucky

This book is printed on acid-free paper that meets the American National Standards Institute Z39.48 standard.

PRINTED IN THE UNITED STATES OF AMERICA

00 01 02 03 04 05 06 07 08 09 — 10 9 8 7 6 5 4 3 2 1

Library of Congress Cataloging-in-Publication Data

Clark, Doris C., 1938–
    Feed all my sheep : a guide and curriculum for adults with developmental disabilities /
Doris C. Clark ; with music by Kinley Lange.— 1st ed.
        p.   cm.
    Includes bibliographical references.
    ISBN 0-664-50113-3 (alk. paper)
    1. Christian education of the mentally handicapped.   I. Title.

BV1615.M37 C53 2000
268′.434′0875—dc21   99-047555

TABLE OF CONTENTS

PART 3 Music for Church Words

Appendix

Suggested Resources

FOREWORD

I had come to this thriving church to preach a stewardship sermon. There were two services back to back. Wow!! How do they do this every Sunday? I was thinking as we went into the second service. Things were moving right along, when I became aware of something unusual. A young man sitting on the aisle near the front of the sanctuary was following the liturgy perfectly, but he wasn't reading what was printed in the bulletin—he was responding in perfect cadence with sounds of his own. Fascinated, I watched him. A look of real joy was on his face as he focused on the worship. Once I had seen him, I began to notice that scattered around on that side of the congregation were a number of other young adults who also seemed to be uniquely challenged. Some followed the service; some just sat. I could tell by looking at the worshipers around them that these special folks must be a regular part of the community.

That experience was my introduction to the Joy Class at First Presbyterian in Austin, Texas. I learned that through the class ten members had been added to the family of that church. Begun by Doris Clark to meet the needs of her son, Tim, this class has opened the door of ministry to many others. Coming from group homes and from Austin State School, up to forty women and men, ranging in age from twenty-five to seventy years old, have participated in the Joy Class. Ten years ago, when I served as church educator in a congregation that decided to respond to the special needs of their Jeff and to his friends, I learned several things:

1. I discovered how very hard it is to find appropriate materials to use in such a class.

2. I witnessed how much it means to these brothers and sisters to be included in church in a way that allows them to be who they are.

3. I learned what a blessing these dear friends can be to a congregation.

It is my prayer that the wisdom of this guidebook and special curriculum will open similar doors of blessing for your congregation.

SYLVIA WASHER
Presbytery Executive, Mission Presbytery

ACKNOWLEDGMENTS

To Tim Clark, who taught us well

To the rest of my family, Don Clark, Amy Clark, and Bethany Detrich, who encouraged me

To the members and staff of First Presbyterian Church, Austin

To Judy Ferguson and the Mission Presbytery Lay Leadership Class of 1990–91

To teachers Pat and Herman Thun, Abby and Clay Ballentine, Kathy Lozano, Dianne Wheeler, Willene and Allen Boger, Carol and John Burgeson, Betty Marshall, Helene Crase, Dawn and Bill Mitchell, Shannon and Michael Shappell, Becky Babb, Mary Burgeson, and Nancy Messenger

To the members of Joy Class, First Presbyterian Church, Austin

To editors Susan Allen, Lee Bowman, Tommie Pinkard, and Millie and Paul Wilson

To Kinley Lange for sharing his musical talent for the Church Words curriculum

To Sylvia Washer for her encouragement and moral support

INTRODUCTION

. . . [Jesus] said to him, ". . . do you love me?" . . . [Peter] said, "Lord, . . . you know that I love you." Jesus said, "Feed my sheep."

—John 21:17 (NIV)

We would like to introduce you to Tim. Tim loves to go to church. He sits in the same pew every Sunday. He attends both Sunday morning worship services because he wants to be sure he sees all his friends. He participates in the liturgy, although he is usually a couple of words behind everyone else.

Tim has been going to church since he was a baby. During his formative years Tim was in church school—in classes with members three or four years younger than he. He was always welcome and always pleased to be there. The greatest problem we had during this early development period was making the teacher aware that it was all right to discipline Tim. The first Sunday he would be in a class, he would get up and wander around the room—doing pretty much as he pleased, while the other children were expected to sit together at group time. New teachers were hesitant to insist that he sit with the group. We finally learned that we must visit with a new teacher before the first Sunday Tim was in her class. He knew what he was supposed to do, but it was great fun for him to see if the teacher did too.

When Tim was graduated from vocational high school at age twenty-one, we began to realize that he no longer "fit" the youth class. He went to young adult discussion groups but there were always problems because of his inability to communicate well and his eagerness to dominate the discussions. Some leaders were good at limiting Tim's participation; others were not.

After years of being in church school, John Timothy found there was no longer a place for him. During the church school hour, he stood outside and visited with whoever happened by.

Tim has Down syndrome.

We are Tim's parents.

Out of personal needs, new ministries are formed. We had the need—a proper class for Tim. What we did not have was information on how to begin, where to look for help, whom to contact, what to ask.

Our search for answers led to the writing of this guidebook so that precious time will not be lost to those in other congregations who wish to begin a class for developmentally disabled adults. This is neither a professional nor a scientific book. It is a practical guide for establishing church classes for the developmentally disabled adult. This guide is intended to help all those "Tims" across the country to have their special place in church school.

DORIS AND DON CLARK

Go therefore and make disciples of all the nations, baptizing them in the name of the Father and the Son and the Holy Spirit, teaching them to observe all that I commanded you; and lo, I am with you always, even to the end of the age. (Matthew 28:19–20)

PART 1
GUIDEBOOK

The Least of These

Look at their faces as they come to us,
Some shy, some frightened, some happy.
We are so noble to be here for them—
We teach, we give hugs, we serve coffee.

Who could have told us the truth we would learn
As we ministered to their needs?
The gifts that they gave us were straight from God's throne.
We were really the ones who had needs.

"Inasmuch as you've done it to the least of these."
This is what Jesus has said.
And we think that the blessings belong to our students.
"The least of these" are those they have fed!

DORIS C. CLARK

ABOUT JOY

Think for a moment about the joy of witnessing a lovely sunset—the myriad changing colors, brilliant to subdued, every hue, every color—filling the western horizon in a breathtaking display.

This is Joy Class.

Joy Class was born in November, 1990, at First Presbyterian Church, Austin, Texas, because of the special needs of one young man. The original members of Joy Class were recruited from a group of his friends. That first Sunday there were three attendees. Now there is an enrollment of thirty-six, with four regular teacher-leaders and four teacher-helpers.

We opened the door and God opened all the windows. The development of this class has been amazing to watch. The need for classes like ours is so great that we have literally had to run to keep up with the demands that met us almost immediately.

Looking back over the years that Joy Class has been in existence, it has been as if God said to us, "You make the space available and put forth the effort to start the class, and I will do the rest."

Teachers have come to us, members of our congregation have volunteered to help in various ways, and our mixture of class members has continued to be conducive to a wonderful learning experience for our students, their teachers, and our congregation.

Through the years that we have experienced Joy Class we have had many times when we have laughed with abandon, or looked at our class members with tear-filled eyes when the emotion of some truth filled us to overflowing. These lovely people are sometimes arrestingly honest in their assessments of life. Following is our attempt to share a few vignettes of our time with Joy.

Gregory

Gregory came through the door of the classroom with two other girls. They were greeted with hugs and hellos. Gregory seemed to enjoy the greeting, but made no effort to return the warmth. Her eyes were fixed on the lines in the floor, as if she were memorizing the pattern. The little smile she managed at first became extremely elusive.

The teachers had thought she might have a hearing problem like the deaf students they had grown accustomed to seeing, but occasionally Gregory responded with a brief smile and a "yes" or a "no." That was all! Her response to the male teacher was avoidance, as much as possible. As the weeks progressed and Gregory came with the other students from the state school, the teachers began to notice something different about her. She was smiling more and more.

On one of those Sunday mornings when everyone was running a little late and several teachers were unable to attend, one teacher arrived to scurry around and try to get the room ready for the students' arrival. The state school bus, of course, arrived early, and as the students came through the door Gregory glanced around the room and said to her teacher, "Are you all alone?"

She then proceeded to help with the preparations.

A small action, but Gregory was blooming, one petal at a time, until she could begin to show her inner beauty to those around her. She had accepted us and, more importantly, she felt accepted by us.

Cleveland

Cleveland was deaf. He began attending Joy Class with his group-home residents shortly after the class began. Cleveland was a slender young man, extremely outgoing and full of exuberance, with an abandon that spoke to the assurance that everyone must love him. His joy was contagious.

After we found a volunteer interpreter, and the residents of Cleveland's group home began attending the worship service, the congregation responded to his enthusiasm with smiles and hugs. He was interested in everyone and everything. He worked in a hospital near the newborn babies, and he was particularly interested in the small children and some of the expectant mothers. He would gleefully tell them that they must be carrying twins.

It was quite an experience for some of our Presbyterian members who were accustomed to everything being done "decently and in order" to share the service with these nonhearing friends.

One Sunday when the sunlight was filtering through the stained-glass windows and casting colored shadows across the quiet congregation, the organist began playing a reverberating piece on the ancient pipe organ. Cleveland began to "hear" or feel the vibrations from the pipe organ. His enthusiasm exploded in a volley of sound.

What an experience! Praise the Lord! The Presbyterians in that service were exposed to pure joy!

Mark

Mark is a wheelchair-bound class member who has cerebral palsy. He is a lovely person whose body just does not cooperate with what he wants to do. He has been attending the worship services at First Presbyterian Church.

One week when Mark attended the worship service, it was Communion Sunday. A church member describes what it was like for her on that Sunday:

> As I sat in the sanctuary and thought about Communion, my attention was drawn to the young man in the row in front of me. It was obvious that he wanted to be a part of the service. It was difficult for him to sit up in his wheelchair and his hands were almost useless as he attempted to grasp the hymnbook.
>
> As the service progressed I watched with interest as the elder who was serving Communion bent down to the young man's level, offering him the bread. As she gazed into those beautiful eyes she said, "The body of Christ, broken for you, Mark."
>
> Tears were streaming down my face as I thought that Mark certainly understood what it meant to have a broken body.
>
> How wonderful it is to allow these new friends to teach us as we worship together.

Bobby

Bobby had come to Joy Class that morning from the state school. She had one thought in mind when she stepped off the bus; to buy a Coke from the machine in the kitchen. After she got her Coke and was seated in the classroom, she paid no attention to the people around her. This was *not* unusual behavior for Bobby. We had just begun to be able to communicate with her, but our efforts produced only limited results.

The group-home residents began to arrive, and excitement reigned. They had brought their new puppy to share with the class. The wiggly, furry brown creature was passed from one class member to another as everyone took turns holding him.

Finally someone placed the puppy on the floor next to Bobby. The puppy, basking in all the attention, jumped up on Bobby's leg. Bobby became extremely agitated and began to scream—loud, excruciating screams—the kind that makes you want to push the "off" button to remove the intruding sound from the air as soon as possible.

Someone grabbed the puppy and took him out!

Tim, another class member, had been observing from across the room. He was immediately at Bobby's side, putting his arm around her and comforting her. He stayed with her until she regained her composure.

What a lovely picture of God's love!

Ricky

For several Sundays the study had focused on self-worth. We had looked at ourselves in mirrors and discussed how we looked. We had talked about personalities and the differences in people. We had talked about characteristics.

As we discussed characteristics, we did a list of things we like about ourselves, and then we did a list of things we wanted to improve about ourselves.

Ricky was having difficulty completing his list and the helper who was working with him was attempting to get him to focus on the project. She said, "Ricky, what are some things about yourself that you would like to change? Are there some things you do that you would like to stop doing, or are there some things you don't do that you would like to start doing?"

Ricky thought for a moment and quickly responded, "I like myself just fine!!"

Can you find one person in another adult church school class who could respond in that fashion?!

Trouble

In the process of developing a class like Joy Class, there are sometimes stories one would just as soon forget. Nevertheless, it is only in analyzing the painful as well as the joyful that we gain insights.

When people are engaged in developing an exciting program, they become unable to understand that others who are not involved in the process may not be as enthusiastic about the program as they are. Once in a while we are "whacked on the head" with that truth.

Joy Class was several months in existence when one of the teachers received a phone call. The call was from a friend of Joy Class who had just been called by an irate church member. This person was apparently engaged in a telephone campaign to remove Joy Class from the worship service because the students were "disruptive."

At this time the class was sitting together in the church service in order to take advantage of the interpreter for the hearing-impaired members. At times we would have as many as ten members seated together for the service.

After tears of disappointment and anxious moments of not knowing how many people might be feeling the same way, and after a slight rearrangement of where the class was seated, we received another call, from a second irate member. She too had been called about the removal of Joy Class from the service. She told the complaining woman that Joy Class was a very important part of our church, and that it was a travesty to try to remove it. She called to tell us that she strongly supported our class. She was indeed a blessing to us at that moment.

We have no idea how many people were called, but we discovered that there were people in our congregation who looked forward to worshiping with Joy Class on Sunday! We were also reminded of the need to keep our congregation informed, and to be concerned about helping our class to learn appropriate behavior for the worship service. Most of our church members have been patient and helpful in this process.

The complaints stopped and Joy Class is still in our worship service.

A Christmas Card

Our church has been greatly blessed to have an artist named Millie as a member. Joy Class was doubly blessed to have Millie do the artwork for the Christmas card they decided to do for the church.

We had been studying the Christmas story, using puppets, a crèche, role-playing, and books, all through the Advent season, and we decided that our Christmas card to the church should include all the parts of the Christmas story.

Millie drew the lovely Victorian scenes of the Christmas story, and the members of Joy Class, using vivid pastel crayons, colored the pictures, working for several Sundays.

This was indeed a labor of love, and their creativity was boundless. We had a redheaded angel and green Wise Men, but motivation is a wonderful thing. The coloring was done with extreme care, and the end result was spectacular.

The card was assembled the Sunday before Christmas, with each scene being carefully placed on the eight-foot Christmas card.

The card was presented to the church during the worship service, and placed on the wall in the foyer so that everyone could see it when they came to the Christmas Eve service.

It is always amazing to watch the members of Joy Class when they are involved in a project. If we could all somehow capture the love, the concern, and the diligence they exhibit, we would be greatly blessed.

Sharing Our Joy (A Hand Dance)

"The Lord's Prayer will be interpreted for us this morning by the members of Joy Class."

It was the pastor's voice during Sunday morning worship. After weeks of studying what the words in the Lord's Prayer meant and practicing the hand and arm movements that were an interpretation of those meanings, we were finally ready to help others in worship.

The congregation was quiet, not knowing what to expect. Thirty Joy Class members rose from their chairs, or rolled forward in their wheelchairs, to take their places at the front of the sanctuary.

As they stood facing the congregation there was no doubt that they had all come for a purpose greater than themselves. They had come to help in worship, and that purpose was reflected in their serious expressions.

The strains of recorded music filled the sanctuary, and suddenly ribbon-bedecked arms were in motion. The dance had begun. A sense of awe and wonder swept over the congregation. The members of Joy Class were presenting their praise to God as one, with a beautiful, creative expression of love and happiness which showed in the radiance of their smiling faces.

There were few dry eyes among the folks who had gathered for worship that day.

The members of Joy Class had accomplished their goal. They had led in worship, and their giving was a sweet offering to God.

Purpose

One of the most striking characteristics of our sanctuary is a collage of stained-glass windows that were lovingly preserved from the old downtown sanctuary and artfully arranged on the west wall of our present sanctuary. Upon entering the room, one is drawn to the beauty of this wall. It is the eye-catcher.

The most symbolic areas of our sanctuary, however, are the stone walls on either end of the room. The many and diverse shapes, colors, and textures of the stones, which are held together with the same mortar, make a strong and beautiful single surface for the end pieces of the room. These stone walls represent strength. They represent "community." We are all beautifully different, and with the mortar of God's love, we are able to make a strong, lovely, united family.

Joy Class is part of the texture of the community we call First Presbyterian Church, Austin. We are proud to be at the leading edge of what is happening in our society, by welcoming the Joy Class members into our midst, to serve them and to be served by them.

What do they get from worship at First Presbyterian? What do any of us gain from being in our church service? Yes—the Bible is read, the Word is proclaimed, voices are raised in song. All these things are important, but the one thing that keeps us all coming back is the sense of community—the joy of sharing in the worship of God with other members of our family. Joy Class members are no different in that respect.

Which brings us to Tim.

Tim is short of stature, approximately five feet, three inches, with balding hair and a friendly demeanor that would put a politician to shame.

Tim has been involved in First Presbyterian since 1979, when he was baptized as an adult. Church is easily the most important part of Tim's life.

Most of his friends are at the church. He attends both services on Sunday morning so that he doesn't miss seeing any of his friends.

Golf is Tim's favorite sport, and the men of the church have a golf tournament a couple of times a year. Tim is the first person to sign up for the tournament. Some of the men take Tim under their wing if his dad is unavailable, and he "plays" golf with the best of them. He usually goes home with a trophy for being the most enthusiastic player. He is best known for playing the ball that is closest to the hole, regardless of its ownership.

Tim derives pleasure and confidence from his friends at church, but many of those people have expressed a fact that often escapes too many of us when we are thinking of ministry to persons with developmental disabilities. And that is that Tim ministers to the needs of his friends each day with his interest in them and his caring, friendly attitude. He is a valid member of First Presbyterian Church.

If we open our hearts to the ones who are seemingly the "least of these," the surprise is that they have many truths to teach those of us whose minds are too busy or too cluttered to see God.

It is our prayer that you too will experience this blessing.

IDENTIFY YOUR NEEDS

If there is an interest in starting a class for adults with developmental disabilities in your church, there must be a reason for that interest. Assuming you already have at least one individual in your congregation who would benefit, go to that person, or to the individual responsible for that person, and ask questions about where other developmentally disabled adults may be found in your community. Ask for parents' or care takers' names and phone numbers.

If you do not have someone in your congregation, contact your local chapter of the ARC (Association for Retarded Citizens), or other similar organizations, tell them your purpose, and request information regarding activities for adults with developmental disabilities. Go to these activities and visit with the people. Call the Mental Health and Mental Retardation office. In many communities it promotes more ongoing recreational programs than the Association for Retarded Citizens. Request a list of those activities and a list of group homes in your area, including addresses, phone numbers, and a contact person, if possible. Write or call the group homes on your list and visit with their supervisors about your class.

Look in the Yellow Pages under "schools," "rehabilitation," "Association for Retarded Citizens," and "Mental Health and Mental Retardation." Speak with the city, county, and state office of the Americans with Disabilities Act (ADA). Tell them what you are planning and ask if they would be willing to poll their clients regarding whether a Sunday church class for developmentally disabled adults would be beneficial to them.

If there is a state school or a private residential school in your area, contact the chaplain and see if a church school class might benefit their residents.

Contact as many parents and persons responsible for adults with developmental disabilities in your community as possible, and ask them these questions:

1. Is your developmentally disabled adult now attending church?

2. Does the church you are now attending offer a Sunday class for adults with developmental disabilities?

3. Are adults with developmental disabilities welcome in the worship service at your church?

4. Would it be beneficial to you to have such a class available in the community?

5. Would transportation be a problem?

6. What is the severity of the disability?

7. What special accommodations might be necessary?

In addition, you might find it helpful to poll other churches in your community to determine what services they offer for adults with developmental disabilities or what services they might want to utilize at your church.

When you have compiled the statistics, you will have a more accurate assessment of the need for your class. However, if you can start a class of this nature with only three members, it will be a good beginning. Expect to grow slowly, but be prepared for rapid growth as well. Two or three group homes can fill up your class.

While contacting people, we discovered numerous families who were not attending church because there was no place for their disabled family member. We found others attending classes that were not designed for their special needs. Generally, we found no classes that specifically focused on the needs of adults over twenty-one with developmental disabilities. We discovered a genuine need and attempted to satisfy that need.

The parameters you will set for your class will be determined by the needs you find in your research. Don't be surprised if those parameters begin to change the first few Sundays you are meeting. Remember, the most important word you will need in your vocabulary is "flexibility."

ENGAGE YOUR CHURCH

"Plan your work and work your plan"—not bad advice, particularly before approaching your church leaders regarding this project.

Record the comments you have gleaned from parents, teachers, social workers, agencies, and potential class members. Be ready to substantiate the need for this class. Think through the needs you have found and formulate what resources would be necessary for your church to begin this ministry.

> What type and size of classroom will be needed?
> How many teachers will be required?
> What qualifications will your teachers need to possess?
> Will you need to ask the congregation for help with the class (e.g., refreshments,
>   "Buddies" during worship service, transportation)?
> Will there be a need for volunteer training classes for members of your congregation?

Contact the chairpersons of church committees that might be impacted by this new ministry (adult programs and Christian education, missions, worship).

Analyze the answers to your interview questions and condense that information into a few major points of impact and emphasis. Keep your proposal to one or two paragraphs, stating what you wish to do and why.

Make an appointment to talk to your director of Christian education, your pastor, your adult Christian education program chair, or the equivalents in your church. Ask if you must get session (governing board) approval to start your class.

Even if it is not necessary, it is still a good idea to see if you can go to the session meeting of your church and tell them about your proposed ministry. The more people with whom you can share this plan, the better. If you have enthusiasm for this program, it will be contagious. When you truly feel the need for this program, your message will be heard.

If you meet with opposition, try to discover the "real" reasons and deal with each objection on an individual basis. If there are fears of the unknown from several persons, invite them to accompany you to one of the planned activities for adults with developmental disabilities. Introduce them to some of your potential class members.

Once you have session or governing board approval, share your plans both formally and informally with your church members every chance you get. Use every method available at your church to make the members aware of your plans: newsletters, concerns of the church (during worship), church bulletins, posters, informal conversation.

Persons with mild retardation can possibly be placed in your regular church school classes, even if a volunteer needs to accompany them for several weeks. This would be good for other church members as well as the person with disabilities, giving the church members an opportunity to see that the disabled person has hopes and dreams, difficulties, insights, prejudices, attributes, and contributions to make just like them. We live in this world together. It is particularly fitting that we learn to relate to one another in our worship experience.

However, if the disability precludes inviting the adult with a disability to regular classes, you should do whatever is necessary to introduce your class members to other members of the church. Invite other members of the church to visit your special class and to participate, involve your class members in the worship service, church dinners, picnics, and other special activities. Your goal is to provide a church home for your class members where they are known, respected, and loved for who they are individually.

SELECT YOUR FORMAT

Pioneers on any frontier must rely on their own resourcefulness, and you are entering a new frontier. Curricula that will completely meet the needs of your class will probably not be found because of the diversity of abilities exhibited by members of a class.

There is not a large selection of literature written specifically for adults with disabilities. The "Suggested Resources" at the end of this book (page 107) lists a number of religious education resources. A brochure entitled *Christian Education Resources for Persons Who Are Mentally Retarded*, from Presbyterian Church U.S.A.'s General Assembly, lists the following three:

1. *The Friendship Series* is a three-year curriculum for youth and adults. This series has a heavy emphasis on biblical content. The series includes themes on "God, the Father," "Jesus, the Savior," and "Simple Teachings about the Church and the Work of the Spirit." It has a group leader's kit, teachers' manuals, and student resource packets. Information and a free sample kit may be obtained from the Christian Reformed Church. (This literature includes much detailed information and many teaching aids. It was our feeling that it was almost overwhelming to new teachers. It emphasizes a one-on-one format.)

2. *Living in Faith* includes fifty-two sessions dealing with various aspects of faith and faith involvement, as well as physical development and sex education. The sessions are designed for use with mildly retarded individuals. The literature could be used as a good teacher resource book. The units are provided in a "stand alone" format, and portions of the study may be used individually. (The content seemed a bit too advanced for our class, but again, use depends on the capabilities of the individual members of your group.)

3. *Special Education Teaching Packet* is available from the Southern Baptist Convention and is prepared quarterly. Through the use of Bible stories, the literature is aimed at developing self-image, getting along with others, and caring for God's world. This literature has two levels: one for children, and one for moderately retarded older youth and adults. The teacher's guide includes plans for a full quarter with teaching pictures, activities, songs, and pupil leaflets that can be duplicated. A sample kit is available for approximately $15.00.

After perusing the literature, we chose one that featured a simple format. It is basically:

Fellowship and Refreshments	10–15 minutes
Group Discussion	35–40 minutes
Worship	10–15 minutes

It is important to keep it simple. Develop only one word, one thought, one idea each Sunday. Find interesting ways to visually stimulate thinking and encourage discussion. Use as many of the senses as possible in each session.

Many of the curricula seem to be written for high-functioning people who might possibly do well in a mainstreaming situation. Only the lower-functioning or special-needs individual should be in a separate class. There is no reason the higher-functioning person should not be in regular church classes.

OTHER RESOURCES

Young Children and Worship, by Sonja M. Stewart and Jerome W. Berryman, from Westminster/ John Knox Press in Louisville, Kentucky. Although this literature is written for small children without disabilities, the lessons utilize class participation and visual presentation and are adaptable for adults with mental disabilities. (Our hearing-impaired class particularly enjoyed this approach.) Information on workshops to learn the application of this curriculum may be obtained from either of the authors.

Our Life in Christ for Special Classes is a curriculum from the Lutheran Church Missouri Synod. It includes six Bible stories and a separate teacher's guide, with life application for special students. Thirteen lessons are provided each quarter.

The Story of God's Love, available from Concordia, is a book of seventy Old and New Testament Bible stories with seventy accompanying pictures.

Bible Story Narratives, by Rev. Walter Baumann, is a collection of thirteen biblical narratives with flannelgraph suggestions plus an original poem relating each Bible story.

Bethesda Lutheran Homes has a wealth of information available to persons involved in Christian education for mentally retarded children and adults. Their quarterly publication *Breakthrough* provides suggested lesson plans, information regarding publications, films, and music books. The publication is provided free of charge to churches.

If you have nonhearing class members, it would be helpful to have an interpreter for your class as well as for the worship service. We had a volunteer for the first few months of our class until her job prevented her from continuing. We were able to get Mental Health and Mental Retardation (MHMR) to provide an interpreter for our worship service, since our nonhearing members were from an MHMR group home and from the state school. Our interpreters came from Travis County Deaf Services. Don't be afraid to ask state and local mental retardation agencies for a list of services they provide, and visit with the group home representatives regarding needs you may have. Networking helps in developing your class just as it does in the workplace.

There are several books on signing that might be helpful to your class staff. Check the "Selected Resources" section in the back of this book for books on signing.

After looking at the various curricula, you may decide to write your own. Keep in mind that adults with developmental disabilities are adults, not children. Some teaching methods used with children are useful, but always try to present your lessons with the *adult* perspective in mind.

Many persons with disabilities have jobs, have problems with relationships, enjoy movies, current events, or sports, and some need help coping with separation from family or friends. Sound familiar? Their scope of understanding may be limited, but their humanity is the same as that of any adult.

We have written a curriculum using the simple one-word-per-lesson development process. It is titled "Church Words," and includes lessons for one year of study. Using the premise that many of the class members have not been in churches or have come from various disciplines, we formulated a list of words they might frequently hear in church. The study includes over thirty lessons and is included with this guidebook.

Curriculum may be used for more than one year. Repetition is a good learning tool for students with mental disabilities. The teachers, however, may grow tired of teaching the same study for more than two years. Some lessons may be expanded to last for two Sundays. If a lesson does not seem to fit a particular group, skip it and move to the next one. Remember that whatever curriculum is used, flexibility must be exercised in its use.

Serve the content of your lessons with large portions of love and respect. Use flexibility in your approach, and remember that the curriculum is designed for the student, not the student for the curriculum. Review frequently to emphasize content.

We serve refreshments during the fellowship time at the beginning of our class. Through trial and error we have discovered that it is best to serve muffins or bundt cake, rather than ultrasweet or high-fat treats. We have even served a fruit tray occasionally. You will need to determine if any of your students must avoid sugar or special sweeteners or have allergies to specific foods. We serve muffins, juice, and coffee (decaf). It is better to have creamer and sweetener in individual packets. Class members have a tendency to use more than needed when they are served in bulk.

A registration form should be completed for each student. A copy of our registration form is in the Appendix. This is to provide you with the student's address and phone number as well as the person to contact in an emergency. Information regarding special needs such as allergies or conditions that you need to know must be included. Birthdays are nice to know so that cards may be sent. You may not be able to get any information regarding an individual's religious background, but it is helpful if you can.

Do not hesitate to ask that a group-home assistant stay with a class member if the person's condition warrants it. (This would apply in cases where seizures are likely, or if a member is having some special difficulty that your staff does not feel comfortable in handling.)

RECRUIT YOUR LEADERS

After deciding your format, you must plan for implementing that format. If you do not already have a coordinator, choose someone for that responsibility. The coordinator should be involved in recruiting leaders for the class.

How many students are you expecting? A minimum number of teachers is two. The reason for having two teachers is so that teachers may rotate according to their schedules. We have discovered that this helps to prevent teacher "burnout" and eliminates the need for substitute teachers most of the time. If you have more than four students you will probably need four teachers. You may wish to have one set of teachers do the planning and teaching every other month. It works better in our class to have quarterly meetings and rotate according to our individual schedules. Assignments are made quarterly and planning is done for the quarter.

There is a debate about qualifications for teaching a class for people with disabilities. There are those who would say that a teacher must be formally trained in special education in order to properly relate to the special needs and problems inherent in the class. However, the most important qualifications, regardless of formal training, are a genuine interest in people, a willingness to learn, a contagious enthusiasm, an uncanny ability to adjust, a knowledge of the scope of God's love, a spirit of love imparted with grace, and an imagination to use innovative ideas to meet special needs quickly. Sounds as if Jesus would do quite nicely!

We are talking about teachers who are *special* people, but you will be amazed at how many of these people are in your congregation when you begin your search. They may even come to you.

When we started our class, which is called Joy Class, we anticipated the same difficulty we had experienced in filling teaching positions when we worked with the children's program. After all, in addition to the usual time constrictions every church member experiences today, we had the added problem of people feeling inadequately trained for a specialized position.

After the plans for Joy Class were announced at the session meeting and several informational items had appeared in the bulletin and newsletter, we were approached by one of our church members. He and his wife were deeply interested in helping with the class. They didn't want to lead the class but they were definitely interested in helping.

They had once lived next door to a family who had a son with Down syndrome and enjoyed the time they had spent with him. They had no formal training in teaching adults with disabilities, but they had ample experience in patience, flexibility, and loving. They had reared four children and had several grandchildren. They were vibrant, interested in numerous activities, and excited about the prospect of helping with Joy Class. They became our teachers for the class and two of the best leaders we could ever have hoped to find.

We asked all the teachers to be present for the first several months and then began the rotation. This helps everyone to become accustomed to working together and will give your program more stability as it progresses. When rotation begins, both teams should use the same literature, and planning sessions should be held at least quarterly to make sure continuity is maintained for the class.

We have used a teacher-leader and one or more teacher-helpers in our class. As students are added to the class, and depending on the needs of those students, additional teachers might be needed.

If your class becomes too large to fit your format, you may want to start a second class. (This is difficult to decide based on numbers alone. Some groups may have too many when they reach eight. Others do just fine with a much larger enrollment and many helpers.) When we had hearing and nonhearing students, we divided Joy Class into two groups. We met together for refreshments and fellowship and divided the group for teaching. When attendance was down we could easily teach all the members in one group. This gave us good flexibility in our program.

We are now meeting in one group, even though we might have as many as twenty to twenty-five members present on some Sundays. Our group has bonded well, and with enough helpers in the class they have remained quite happy as a single, cohesive group.

It is important to let your prospective teachers know what the job requires of them. Never twist an arm when recruiting. It will not work to your advantage.

We began to look at the active people in our church, and to assess personalities and abilities to determine whether or not they would fit our needs. There was a young couple, outgoing, friendly, and very involved in our church. At first we were hesitant to approach them about teaching, because we felt they were already doing so much. We have always believed, however, that people should have an opportunity to make their own decisions. We asked them about Joy, and much to our pleasure they were enthusiastic about joining us.

It is difficult to get on the phone and recruit, but phoning remains a very good way to enlist teachers. Compile a list of likely prospects. As your class becomes more visible in the church you will be able to identify the people who seem most interested in helping. Listen as members of your congregation discuss other members. Talk to the people responsible for new-member contact. See if any of the new members have indicated an interest in teaching or have an interest you might use in your class. It is helpful to have at least one male teacher-leader or teacher-helper to assist the men with restroom needs and at least one female teacher to assist the women.

After you have a list of prospects, begin calling. Be prepared to explain what you are doing, what you need them to do, and something about the time they will be expected to serve. Be enthusiastic! Tell them about the students you expect. Again, *don't beg or use a hard sell!* It will not work! You must have teachers who genuinely want to do what they are doing.

In addition to the teachers and helpers for your class, it is advisable to develop a group of class "Buddies." You will be able to use as many Buddies as you can get. These people can be in the class one Sunday or all year. Buddies are in the class primarily for fellowship with the persons with disabilities and to help with whatever class needs there may be on a given Sunday. They can provide friendship, examples of how to behave in class and at church, or extra hands when they are needed. No special training is necessary—just love and willingness to help. Buddies simply come to the class occasionally, or they may sit with a class member in worship or provide transportation or refreshments.

Some possible jobs for Buddies are:

> Attending classes and visiting with the members
> Sitting with class members during worship, helping them learn appropriate
>   behavior, and being aware of their leaving and returning to the service
> Waiting with a class member until transportation arrives after church
> Introducing class members to other members of the congregation
> Bringing and/or serving refreshments to the class
> Helping with special functions for fellowship and fun
> Helping financially with special needs

Recruit Buddies from the congregation through announcements during worship hour, in the church newsletter, or in a special insert in the church bulletin that volunteers sign and place in the offering plate. Be sure they know this does not have to be an every-Sunday job.

Many people in our church have wanted to know how they might help with this ministry. The Buddies group is a great way to involve them.

You will find it helpful to prepare job descriptions for the positions you are trying to fill. This helps the recruiter as well as the person being recruited to know what the position requires. Following are the job description suggestions for your class coordinator, class teacher-leader, and class teacher-helper.

JOB DESCRIPTION FOR CLASS COORDINATOR

—Must be enthusiastic about this program, and be able to share that enthusiasm with others and keep the church informed as to the progress of the class.

—Be willing to educate the congregation regarding persons with developmental disabilities, whether holding group discussions or workshops within the church or correcting misunderstandings, misconceptions, or fears regarding the class.

—Be factual and nondefensive but firm in your responses to questions regarding your class.

—Organize the program and be flexible enough to reorganize when the situation demands.

—Utilize personnel to best advantage for the group.

—Delegate coordination of specific aspects of the program, appointing, for example, a refreshment coordinator, transportation coordinator, training coordinator, Buddy coordinator.

—Recruit teachers, helpers, resource people as needed.

—Conduct or provide training sessions for leaders and helpers. Answer questions that leaders may have regarding class members or class implementation, and be willing to research those questions if the answers are not readily available.

—Order any resources needed for your program in time for the leaders to become familiar with them. This applies also to any music resources they plan to use. (Ordering information is in the back of this book.)

—Be familiar with programs that are available in the community for adults with developmental disabilities, and be prepared to utilize any services that may be helpful to the implementation of the class.

—Search for new literature and information from all sources and evaluate it for use in your class.

—Coordinate class participation in church activities.

—Schedule resource people for special needs, such as sign language interpreters.

—Be available on Sunday morning to help class leaders. See that refreshments are in place. Make sure all class members find their class and are welcomed.

—Be the contact person for the class, and be available to take phone inquiries during the week.

—Keep records of class members and see that a registration form is kept on each member. (See Appendix, "Joy Class Registration.")

—Make sure members are sent cards or are contacted when they are not in the class on Sunday or if there has been a joy or a loss in their lives.

—Keep in touch with the supervisors of the group homes or state schools where class members live. If class members from one home have not been present for two weeks, call their supervisor to see why they have been absent. Frequent personnel changes require constant contact to ensure that members will continue to be brought to class.

JOB DESCRIPTION FOR TEACHER-LEADER

—Be flexible. No matter how many plans are made or training sessions attended, there will be situations that are not anticipated.

—Attend training sessions and be willing to learn as you teach.

—Prepare a lesson for each Sunday for which you are responsible. Be able to adapt each lesson to the needs of your class.

—Attend planning sessions with other leaders. Be familiar with teaching plans for other teams as well as for your own.

—Be at church at least twenty minutes before the class begins in order to have the room arranged and everything in place. Make the room look inviting and ready for your class members when they arrive. Be ready to greet each class member when he or she arrives, and visit with each one individually.

—Learn about the needs of each member.

—Sit with those who need special attention during the worship service, or help prepare a class Buddy to do so.

—Be prepared to supervise helpers during class.

JOB DESCRIPTION FOR TEACHER-HELPER

—Be flexible. No matter how many plans are made or training sessions attended, there will be situations that are not anticipated.

—Attend training sessions and be willing to learn as you teach.

—Be familiar with the lesson for each Sunday, and be willing to participate as the teacher-leader requests.

—Prepare name tags and keep attendance records. Make sure each new member is given a registration form and collect those forms when they are completed. (Generally the blank forms are taken to the home to be filled out and returned the following Sunday.) Maintain these forms in a member notebook that is kept in the classroom. If there is more than one teacher-helper, this may be a designated responsibility for one person.

—Arrive early to help get the room ready and greet early arrivals.

—Visit with class members.

—Be ready to help with the teaching projects, misunderstandings, and rest-room needs.

—Sit with those who need special attention during the worship service, or help prepare a class Buddy to do so.

—Be prepared to supervise helpers during class.

Remember—enthusiasm and flexibility!!

PUBLICIZE YOUR CLASS

Aim for your target!

During the process of determining the need for your class, you will have made some contacts who can help to spread the word. But just relying on word of mouth is not good enough! You must get the information into the hands of the people responsible for the adults you are trying to reach.

If you have a list of people you have interviewed, mail a letter to those people letting them know when your class is beginning and what your study will encompass.

Call your MHMR office and ask for their family and community support section. Request a list of group homes in your city. If they do not have such a list, keep asking questions until they give you a number where you can get the information you need. There may be a Directory of Services book that is published annually. If there is one for your area, you can request that they send it to you. Sometimes you must be persistent. Some MHMR offices have an MR Facts phone line that gives weekly information about services that are available in the community. Get your class included on that list. Ask if they have newsletters and if information about your class could be included.

Prepare an information letter about your class, and mail it to all the group homes on your list. Include a contact person or persons and phone numbers so that the supervisors of the group homes may reach you for information.

Some newspapers have a church news section. There is usually a charge to have your church included, but this is a good way to advertise your class. If you talk to the church news editor, you might be able to get the newspaper to do a feature story about your class after you get it started.

Publicizing your class within your church is also important. Talk about the class when you are with other members. Write articles for your newsletter and bulletin. Speak to the congregation about special needs during your "Concerns of the Church" or your announcement period during worship services.

Invite members of the congregation to visit your class. One way to do that is to invite church school classes for adults and children to visit your class. Your congregation must see that teaching and learning is happening in your class. They need to have the opportunity to feel the happiness and love that prevail in your class. They need to see that your class members are people with hearts, souls, achievements, and joy, not just problems.

Fears and objections are put to rest through knowledge and understanding. Help your church members to obtain that knowledge and understanding whenever and however you can.

Special informational articles regarding issues and facts about developmentally disabled adults could be included in your newsletter on a regular basis. If your church has a specific time for special classes, such as Wednesday evenings, you might lead an informational class or have a guest speaker lead a workshop to inform your congregation about some aspect of developmental disability or to do a class on sign language if you have class members who need signing. Some informational videos are available from Bethesda Lutheran Homes and Services, and are on-loan free to churches. See "Suggested Resources" for contact information.

Do not be surprised if your enrollment changes from time to time. When you are dealing with group homes and people who are relying on others for their transportation, attendance can be sporadic or stop abruptly. Maintain a list of your group homes, with the supervisors' names and phone numbers, and keep in touch with them. Make them aware of any attendance problems you may be having. If you lose members, simply begin your recruitment process again.

Keep in mind that one or two group homes can give you six to twelve members all at once. Be prepared for the increased staff needs you may have as a result of your recruitment efforts. The need for church classes is definitely there.

Be prepared!

CONTINUE YOUR EFFORTS

Determining whether new members are compatible with your existing class can be tricky. Be open to the possibility of beginning a second class if the need arises. As you grow, protect your existing class, but be open to ways you may be able to serve a new group if they do not mix with the present group. We have found that a wide variety of individual needs can be met in a common classroom.

We did find it necessary to divide our class, however, when we had hearing and nonhearing members. Our particular nonhearing members were more limited than our hearing members. Otherwise, the two groups would have been compatible.

You may be asked to accept children in your adult class. Many times children can be included in the regular church program in a younger class than their chronological age. Depending on the severity of their disability, you may need to find a helper who will provide one-on-one assistance for the child in a regular classroom. This provides normal interaction with other children and is generally a beneficial learning experience for the regular children as well as for the new child. We have found that it is not the best arrangement to have children and adults in the same class. Their needs are different and something is sacrificed for one or the other if they attempt to meet together.

If some members are disruptive and prevent others from enjoying their class, you may want to consider removing those members from the class and teaching them in a separate class with more individual attention. If their behavior and ability to interact improves, they might be able to rejoin the others. If not, they would still be able to have a part in the worship experience by having a separate class more suited to their needs.

Our experience has been that most of our members interact well. If one is occasionally disruptive, it doesn't last very long. So far we have not had to consider pulling anyone out for behavioral reasons.

Generally, the group homes, state homes, parents, or guardians are eager to work with class leaders in getting any problems of adjustment solved. As you can imagine, communication is of utmost importance.

Some of our class members attend the worship service. We are in a continual learning experience regarding worship. We frequently talk about our manners during worship, and why it is important to think about the other worshipers.

Be sure your helpers or Buddies understand that it is all right to say "No" to a class member if respect for their adulthood is maintained. Most adults with developmental disabilities want to cooperate and please their friends, but sometimes there is confusion about what is expected.

If any of your class members have special problems, such as bladder control, it is helpful to inform their Buddy in case there is an urgent need to leave during worship.

We have a rest room break between class and worship, and try to encourage everyone to take advantage of the opportunity. Most class members do well during worship, after they learn that we try to avoid leaving during the service. We have learned to limit the number of drinks we enjoy during refreshment time and the amount of sugar we consume. (Drinks are removed after everyone has been served.)

We have had one class member who could not sit through the service without going to the rest room. We confirmed with his group home leader that he did indeed have a bladder problem. It is helpful to know about any such problems when the class member is registered.

Familiarize yourself with the other special classes that are offered on Sunday in your city. If you recruit someone who will not benefit from your class, perhaps there is another class in another church that addresses those needs. If not, you may want to consider expanding your ministry.

As we see more and more adults with developmental disabilities being placed in group homes instead of institutions, the call for community services to meet their needs becomes increasingly urgent. We, as the church, must be ready to respond to that call and provide Christian education to these brothers and sisters.

More churches must respond to this need. The rewards of getting to know these people, who for too long have been segregated from us, are overwhelming. It takes work and dedication to provide this service, but the blessings are there for those who are willing to make the effort.

SHARE YOUR JOY

Your congregation will want to help you toward a successful program. They will not always volunteer, but they will agree to help if they are asked. One of the responsibilities of leading this program is providing ideas for congregational involvement and mission. The possibilities are endless, and we challenge you to be creative.

We suggest below a few possibilities for service, both for your class members and for your congregation. Some ideas require limited involvement; others require an extensive commitment of time and resources.

1. Provide a chart for the congregation to sign to bring refreshments. A refreshment coordinator wouldbe helpful so that teachers would not have to spend time organizing that program

2. Establish a "worship Buddies" program to encourage church members to adopt two or three class members and to sit with them during worship. This would require the church member to visit the class, meet the class members, and be responsible for them during the service. If the Buddy will not be present on a given Sunday, he or she would be responsible for finding a substitute. Some training would be desirable.

3. Volunteer some of your class members and a helper to be greeters one Sunday. (Greeters stand at the entry door before the worship service to welcome worshipers as they enter.) This is a lovely way for class members to meet the congregation.

4. Encourage the members of your congregation to become advocates for developmentally disabled adults. Your local MHMR office can give you information about this program. An advocate helps the disabled person to live independently by providing guidance with financial management and help with the business of everyday living.

5. Start a job bank for disabled adults. Encourage business persons in your congregation to provide jobs for them.

6. Encourage your church members to volunteer at a state school. The schools provide training programs for volunteers that would be helpful for your class staff members to take as well.

7. Encourage volunteering at MHMR to help with their programs.

8. Establish a group of Buddies to provide transportation for class members who cannot come to church without a ride.

9. Encourage your class members to come to special programs at the church such as church picnics, dinners, and Christmas parties. Enlist members of the congregation to be Buddies for your class members who attend special events.

10. Volunteer your class members to help serve special breakfasts or meals at the church. Be sure to check with group home leaders, parents, or advocates to see if their people can be present for such activities before committing them.

11. Encourage groups within the church to sponsor special activities for your class such as bowling, miniature golf, a dance, or some special performance such as the *Nutcracker* ballet at Christmastime.

12. Communicate with your pastor regarding ways the class could participate in a worship service.

Ready, Set, Go!!

PART 2

CHURCH WORDS:
A CURRICULUM

WORDS FOR TEACHERS AND HELPERS

(Get ready to be taught. We need our students more than they need us.)

Flexibility: The ability to bend, stretch, adjust, and realign with amazing grace and ease

Love: An expression of inner beauty and wisdom that comes straight from the heart of God through his most unlikely messengers

Joy: A celebration of life as it is with no "what ifs" or "if onlys"

Patience: The ability to scrap a lesson you have worked very hard to prepare and join the class where they happen to be at the time. The ability to smile and be calm when the behavior you had worked so hard to change is suddenly back in the middle of the worship service

ABOUT THE CLASS

Teachers should plan to arrive at least twenty to thirty minutes before class time (you may want to designate who will arrive thirty minutes before). Sometimes there are early arrivers, and it is good to have a teacher available for them. The teachers for the day will be responsible for getting the refreshment table ready (mixing the juice concentrate, setting out the coffee, creamer, sweetener, cups, napkins, plates, and muffins). It is nice to have a plastic cloth to put on the table. If you have someone in your church who will help by being your refreshment coordinator, the muffins and juice will be provided by church members and the teachers will not have that responsibility. Church members should be given as many opportunities to help with your class as possible.

Each Sunday session will begin with all class members together for fellowship and refreshments for approximately ten to fifteen minutes, depending on when they arrive. Refreshments should be removed after the fifteen-minute period. During this time it is good for everyone to get a name tag. You may want to make them ahead of time so that you simply have to put them on the class members when they arrive. Name tags with plastic jackets and pins may be reused each Sunday, reducing expense and waste of paper. A bulletin board works well as a holder for the name tags.

After everyone has been greeted, had refreshments, and visited with friends, begin the class time. Depending on the needs of your class, you may wish to divide into smaller groups, or you may find that they enjoy staying in one large group with one teacher-leader and several teacher-helpers. You may want to let the members decide on a name for their group. The class time will be thirty- to forty-five minutes in length.

It may be helpful to light a candle when it is class time. Class members seem to enjoy the use of symbolism, and the candle will come to mean it is time to study or a time to learn about God. Light the candle quietly and with purpose. Explain that when the candle is lighted it is time for us to be in class and to learn about God. The teacher should begin by lighting the candle for the first several sessions and then take turns having class members light the candle. Don't forget to extinguish the candle at the close of the class. The long fireplace matches work best for this activity.

If you have readers in your class, let them help if they can when you have a scripture verse to read. If there are no readers, mark the scripture with a bookmark and highlight the verse so that a nonreader may find the verse for you. Allow the class members to help with cleanup. They enjoy feeling useful. Make sure the members who are staying for the worship service go to the rest rooms at the end of the session.

You may wish to use a poster board with the outline of a church on it. Each Sunday a class member may put the Church Word the class studied inside the church. These will remain displayed in the room until the study is complete.

Bible stories are not used for every lesson. When there is a Bible story, it should be told as a story using any visual material you wish. NEVER read the entire story from the Bible. The Bible references are for you to understand the story. Flannelgraphs, puppets, storybooks with pictures, teaching pictures, videos, or dramatizations may be used. Parts of the scripture may be read to emphasize part of the story, but some visual stimulation is necessary to keep the attention of your class for the whole of the story.

If you do not have their attention, it is of little value to tell the story. Suggestions are made for many of the lessons in this study to be developed into two-session lessons, depending on how much of the material is used and how much interest the class exhibits. The lessons may be used in the order they appear or moved to fit the needs of your class. You may wish to use only the lessons that pertain to a certain portion of the church year. The material is flexible. An example: Use the lessons for "Christian," "Cross," "Baptism," "Communion," "Holy Spirit," and "Church Membership" as a confirmation study, culminating in baptism and church membership for those students who wish it. Visit with your pastor regarding baptism and church membership. Many of your class members are capable of making the commitment to adult church membership and should be accepted as such.

Review is extremely important. Find ways to review what has been taught previously.

Singing is an important part of the class time. Most of the students enjoy singing and become familiar with the songs if they are repeated frequently. Songs may always be used to fill in time if the class time seems to be dragging. If you do not have a pianist-singer or guitarist-singer in your class, you may wish to have your church musician do a tape of some of the songs you will be using in class. The songs should be recorded at a slightly slower tempo for learning. Teach the music one line at a time, letting them listen to a line and then singing it with them, gradually adding another line until the song is learned. Then sing the song in its entirety several times during the session (only if they seem to enjoy the song). A keyboard is good to have if you have someone who plays, and your class members will enjoy having percussion instruments to play occasionally. A music section is provided following the curriculum section of this book, and some of the lessons will include songs from that section.

Hymns are good to use, so that your class will be familiar with them in the church service. It would be good to have some of your church hymnals available in your classroom and practice finding the hymns to sing. Some song suggestions are made in some of the lessons and are listed under "Music for Church Words" on page 85. Check for your music needs ahead of time so that you will be able to order music, if necessary, and have someone record it for you.

Prayer time is a time for bonding among class members. It is an exciting thing to see members begin to share and pray for each other. It is good to have a prayer to close the class as you stand in a circle and hold hands. Discuss who and what the group will include in their prayer at the beginning of the class. Writing the prayer topics on the board in a list is a good way to remember what to include in the prayer. Before long class members will begin to come to the class with their prayer requests ready.

You can soon judge if any persons with mild retardation can be placed in your regular church school classes, even if a volunteer needs to accompany them for several weeks. As we stated in Part 1, this would be good for other church members as well as for the person with disabilities, giving the church members an opportunity to see that the disabled person has hopes and dreams, difficulties, insights, prejudices, attributes, and contributions to make just like them. We live in this world together. It is particularly fitting that we learn to relate to one another in our worship experience.

If, however, the disability precludes inviting the adult with disabilities to regular classes, you should do whatever is necessary to introduce your class members to other members of the church. Invite other members of the church to visit your special class and to participate; involve your class members in the worship service, church dinners, picnics, and other special activities. Prepare your class members for church membership. Your goal is to provide a church home for your class members where they are known, respected, and loved for who they are individually.

LESSON 1: FELLOWSHIP

Definition:

A group of people with a common goal who are bound together with love—like a family. Also, the bonding activities engaged in by a group of people with a common goal

Bible Story:

Acts 2:42–47. The Early Church Eating Together (This story could be done with stick puppets.)

Scripture:

1 John 4:21

Preparation:

1. If you are going to take pictures of all the class members, be sure you have a camera and film. A Polaroid is good. It is nice, however, to have two copies of the pictures. That way you can give one to the class member and put one on the class poster marked "Fellowship." The poster will remain on display, and pictures of new members can be added as they come.

2. If you are going to make no-bake cookies or candies to share with church members during coffee fellowship, be sure you have your recipe and all the ingredients and utensils. Some towelets are helpful for before and after preparation. Make sure there is a tray or plate to serve them.

Development:

1. Write the word FELLOWSHIP on the board or chart tablet. Ask if the class knows what it means. Say the word. Give a brief definition.

2. Ask, "Do you need more than one person for FELLOWSHIP?"

3. Talk about friends.

   - "Who is your best friend?"
   - "What makes this person your friend?"
   - "What are some things you do with your friend?"
   - "How do you feel when you are with your friend?"

4. Ask, "Does FELLOWSHIP involve fun?"

5. Talk about fun.

   - "How do you have fun?"
   - "Can you have fun with someone else? with many people?"
   - "How can you tell if someone is having fun?"

6. Read 1 John 4:21.

7. Talk about love.

   - "How do we show love to someone?"
   - "If we love someone, do we like to be with that person?"
   - "How do you treat someone you love?"

8. Ask, "Could we say that FELLOWSHIP includes all these things we just talked about? What were they?" (Friends, fun, love)

9. Sing "Reach Out" (*Music in Special Religious Education,* page 6).

10. Give everyone a sheet of paper and write the word FELLOWSHIP at the top. This could be done with dots or pencil that they may trace over. Have them put one hand on the paper and trace around it. Then draw people heads on each of the fingers. (They can take it home today or keep it in a folder to take home later.)

11. The scripture story is about the early church and the things they did together, such as eating meals, caring for those who were sick, and helping those who were poor. As the story is told, use your imagination as to how they lived and related to one another in love. Don't be afraid to have fun with it. Use puppets or do a dramatization, letting class members help.

12. At this point you may want to let them decorate their FELLOWSHIP poster. If you began taking their pictures during their fellowship time, you can continue to do so and explain that the pictures will go on the poster so that anyone who comes in our room will know that we have fellowship with one another. Another option is to ask if they would like to prepare some treats for the other church members and share with them at the fellowship time before or after the worship service. If there is time, you may wish to do both options by making this lesson a two-session lesson.

13. If you have made treats, decide who will serve those.

14. Have your closing time together, thanking God for the fellowship we feel with one another and with the rest of the church.

LESSON 2: SANCTUARY

Definition:

A place set aside for the worship of God. Also, a room or area where the community gathers to worship

Bible Study:

1 Kings 5–9; 2 Chronicles 2–7. The Building of the Temple

Scripture:

Psalm 122:1

Preparation:

1. Borrow a dollhouse from someone if you do not have one. If you can't find one, gather pictures of different rooms in a house.

2. Prepare a cardboard box. Leave it open at the top and on one side so that the class can see the interior.

   A. If there are stained-glass windows in your church, prepare small geometric-shaped pieces of colored construction paper and window-shaped pieces of white paper. Class members may glue the shapes on the white paper windows to simulate stained glass and then glue the windows in the box sanctuary.

   B. If you have pews or chairs, prepare construction paper replicas by folding pieces of paper, leaving a base where class members will put glue, and install them in your box.

   C. Prepare a cross if there is one in your sanctuary. (Choose several interesting characteristics of your sanctuary and prepare an activity that will duplicate those characteristics in your box sanctuary. Have several items already placed, and allow the class to do a small part of the assembly.)

Development:

1. Talk about homes. Let the class look at the dollhouse.

2. Ask, "Are there any special rooms in the house?"

   - "Where do you cook in the house?"
   - "Where would you go when it is time to sleep?"
   - "Where would you take a bath or a shower?"
   - "Where would you sit at a table and eat?"

3. Say, "So there are special rooms in a house. You could do these things we discussed in other rooms, but there are rooms that are made for special activities."

4. Say, "Let's think about our church building. Are there special rooms here?"

   Respond to their suggestions or help them think—church school room, fellowship hall, nursery.

5. If they don't suggest SANCTUARY, introduce the word. Write the word on the board or a chart tablet. Say the word. Ask them to say the word or sign the word.

6. Ask if anyone knows where this special place is in our church.

7. Define SANCTUARY for them.

8. Show them the cardboard box you have prepared.

9. Say, "We are going to think of some of the special things about our sanctuary."

10. Ask, "What is something you remember about our sanctuary?"

    (As they name things they remember, place your replicas (see "Preparation," above) in the box. Let each member help with making or installing one item in the box sanctuary. You may need two box sanctuaries if your group is large.

11. Tell the story. Say: "There is a Bible story that tells about a time when a new temple was built. A temple was a special place to worship God, and in it there was a room for that worship much like our sanctuary."

12. Read today's scripture, or let one of the class members do it.

13. Have a closing prayer.

14. Sing "I Was Glad" ("Music for Church Words" section, page 91).

15. Say, "We are going to the sanctuary now for worship. Be sure to look at our sanctuary and see what special things you can see this morning."

LESSON 3: WORSHIP

Definition:

The expression of love and honor to God

Bible Story:

Matthew 18:19–20

Scripture:

Matthew 18:20

Preparation:

1. Provide worship bulletins and highlighting pens for class members to use.

2. Gather pictures of people singing, reading scripture, praying, preaching, and so on.

3. Use "I Was Glad" ("Music for Church Words" section, page 91). Or: Use "I Will Worship and Bow Down" (*Music in Special Religious Education,* page 12).

Development:

1. Write the word WORSHIP on the board or chart tablet.

2. Say, "Today our word is WORSHIP."

3. Ask if anyone knows what the word means. (There may or may not be responses.)

4. Say, "WORSHIP is what we do when we go to church in the SANCTUARY. When we worship we show our love and respect for God." You may wish to review SANCTUARY briefly from Lesson 2.

5. Pick up a bulletin and say, "This bulletin contains the Order of Worship for today. This is what we will be doing in our worship service today."

6. Say, "We are going to make a list of some things we do when we worship." Show the class the pictures of people singing, reading the Bible, praying, preaching.

7. As they identify each activity, write the name of the activity on the board or chart tablet under WORSHIP and place the picture next to the name of the activity. You may want to let a student place each picture.

8. Help them look in their bulletin to see if the activity is included. When the activity is found, use highlighting pens to mark it.

9. Sing "I Was Glad" ("Music for Church Words" section, page 91). You may also want to sing one stanza of one of the hymns listed in the bulletin.

10. Ask if the class can think of other things we do in worship.

11. Ask, "Can we worship in places other than the sanctuary?"

12. Say, "Let's plan our own worship service. What should we do first?" Use the pictures on the board or chart tablet to remind them.

   A. Light a candle.

   B. Sing a praise song, such as "Psalm 100" ("Music for Church Words" section, page 93) or "I Was Glad" ("Music for Church Words" section, page 91).

   C. Read Matthew 18:20.

   D. Say a prayer.

13. Say, "We will be going to worship now. Let's remember what worship is and we can all show our love for God today."

Note: This lesson might provide the opportunity to discuss "etiquette for the worship service." Your class may need to be reminded occasionally about appropriate behavior in the service. Keep the discussion positive and explain why it is good to follow each rule. It is great to use puppets to talk about behavior problems. It is better for the puppet to instruct regarding behavior than to have a teacher do so.

LESSON 4: PASTOR

Definition:

A person who is chosen by God to care for and instruct God's people

Bible Story:

Matthew 4:18–22

Scripture:

John 21:15–17

Preparation:

1. Gather pictures of people doing various jobs. Be sure to include workers such as janitors, store personnel, office workers, as well as the usual policeman, fireman, and the like.

2. Be sure to have a picture of your pastor in robe or Sunday attire.

3. Provide a poster board or mural paper and Plas-ti-tak or glue.

4. Invite your pastor to come and talk to the class about his or her job.

5. Make photocopies of the pastor's picture with PASTOR printed at the top of the paper and the pastor's name under the picture.

Development:

1. Have the pictures of workers on the table when members arrive. Allow them to look at the pictures for a while.

2. Let members come forward one at a time and hold a picture so that the others may see. Ask the class if they can tell what job the person in each picture is doing.

3. As the jobs are identified, have the class member who is holding the picture put it on the poster or mural paper.

4. Ask the class members what kinds of jobs they have. Engage them in some discussion about what they are expected to do at work. This might be a good time to talk about some good work habits.

5. Show the class a picture of the pastor wearing a robe and stole (if appropriate). Ask if they know who he or she is.

6. Say, "This is our pastor, _____."

7. Write the word PASTOR on the board or chart tablet.

8. Say, "A pastor is a person who is chosen by God to care for and teach God's people."

9. Ask, "What are some of the things a pastor has to do?"

10. If your pastor is available at this time, ask him or her to talk to the class about the pastor's job. (You may need to rearrange the lessons to accommodate your pastor's schedule.) Be sure the class thanks the pastor for coming.

11. Make a list of the pastor's responsibilities on the board or chart tablet.

12. Read the scripture or tell the story, or you may want to do both.

13. Say, "The pastor stands behind the pulpit to preach during the worship service. Let's pretend this is our pulpit. Who would like to be the pastor today and preach to us?"

14. Encourage members to stand at the "pulpit" and say one thing.

15. Distribute pictures of the pastor to each class member to put in the member's folder.

16. Join hands and say, "We are glad that God loves us enough to provide a pastor to teach us and help us." Prepare a prayer list if you have not done so, and pray for those items. Be sure to include your pastor in your prayer.

17. Sing "Our Pastor" ("Music for Church Words" section, page 92).

LESSON 5: CHOIR/CHOIRMASTER

Definitions:

> CHOIR—the group of people who sing special music in the worship service and lead the congregation in singing hymns

> CHOIRMASTER—the person who leads the choir and provides the music for the worship services (may be the organist)

Scripture:

> Psalm 66:1–2

Preparation:

1. Provide choir robes for each member. Before Sunday get permission from the choirmaster to borrow the robes, and be sure to return them in the same condition and on time.

2. Arrange for the choirmaster to drop by for a visit on Sunday, if possible. If this is not feasible, have a picture of your choirmaster and/or organist and choir available.

3. Find pictures of groups of people, for example, dancers, a football team, family.

Development:

1. Show pictures of groups one at a time. Encourage discussion of who these people are, what they are doing, and where they are.

2. Say, "Today we are going to talk about a group of people who help us to worship. We call this group the CHOIR."

3. Write CHOIR on the board or chart tablet.

4. Ask, "Does anyone know what the choir does?"

5. Ask, "How does the choir look?"

6. Say, "We have some choir robes here today. Let's put them on and see how they feel." If there are not enough robes to accommodate everyone, have them take turns being "the CHOIR."

7. Suggest that they sing a hymn they enjoy singing—perhaps "Amazing Grace" (found in most church hymnals; for example, see *The Presbyterian Hymnal,* number 280).

8. Ask, "Who will lead us? Who usually leads the choir when they sing?"

9. Write CHOIRMASTER on the board or chart tablet. Tell them your choirmaster's name and write it on the board.

10. If the choirmaster is available, introduce him or her. Let the choirmaster tell the class about his or her job. The class may have questions.

11. When the choir director has left, say, "Who would like to be the CHOIRMASTER and lead our song?"

12. Let them take turns leading the choir. Have several suggestions of hymns for singing, or use some songs they have sung in past lessons.

13. Have one of the class members find the scripture. (Have it marked with a bookmark and highlighted.)

14. Read the verses or allow a reading class member to do so. Nonreaders enjoy finding the verse.

15. Join hands and sing "Blest Be the Tie That Binds" (found in most church hymnals; for example, see *The Presbyterian Hymnal,* number 438).

16. Have a closing prayer.

Note: If the choirmaster comes, take time from whatever you are doing to introduce him or her to the class. Sometimes Sunday morning schedules make it difficult to time the visit correctly.

LESSON 6: HYMN/HYMNAL

Definitions:

HYMN—a song that is sung in worship

HYMNAL—the book that contains the hymns or songs that we sing in worship

Scripture:

Psalm 89:1; Psalm 92:1; Psalm 95:1–2

Preparation:

1. Have a hymnal and Bible available for each member.

2. Bring tapes of hymns and other kinds of music and a tape player.

3. If a keyboard is available, have it in the classroom.

4. Have several kinds of ads for music and pictures of people singing, dancing, and enjoying music.

5. Provide some rhythm instruments.

Development:

1. Have tape recorder, tapes, and rhythm instruments on the table when members arrive.

2. Allow them to listen to portions of several tapes and play with the instruments.

3. Have pictures on the table for everyone to see. Nonhearing members will need to see the pictures, as they will be unable to hear the tapes.

4. Ask, "What is your favorite kind of music?"

5. Ask, "Do you have a favorite singer?" Allow time for discussion. They may want to sing one of their favorite songs.

6. Say, "There is a special kind of music that we sing on Sunday during the worship service. Does anyone know what that music is called?"

7. Say, "We call these songs HYMNS." Write HYMN on the board or chart tablet.

8. Ask, "Where can we find these hymns?"

9. Give each member a hymnal and ask if anyone has heard the word HYMNAL.

10. Write HYMNAL on the board or chart tablet.

11. Say, "There is a book in the Bible where hymns can be found. It is the songbook of the Bible. Does anyone know what book it is?" (Psalms) Help the class find Psalms in their Bibles. Show them that Psalms is located in the middle of the Bible.

12. Ask if anyone has a favorite HYMN.

13. If there are favorites, have someone play several on the keyboard. The deaf members might put their hands on the keyboard to feel the vibrations.

14. Sing one of the hymns. If you have hearing-impaired members, arrange for someone to do the signing for them so that they can sing with the group.

15. Sing it again and use the instruments. (Make sure the doors are closed.) Sing as many hymns as time permits.

16. Let someone find one of today's scripture passages that has been marked in the Bible.

17. Close the lesson by reading the scripture and saying a prayer.

LESSON 7: STEWARDSHIP/OFFERING

Definitions:

> STEWARDSHIP—the management of all one's resources for the betterment of God's world

> OFFERING—often used in connection with one's money and how it is given to the church

Bible Story:

> Mark 12:41–44

Scripture:

> 2 Corinthians 9:7

Preparation:

1. Provide several small items of merchandise for members to "buy" (small packages of M&M's, stickers, marking pens, buttons, for example).

2. Have enough pennies to give each member five.

3. Bring a piggy bank, a bankbook, an offering plate, a movie ad, some food.

4. Have pictures of the pastor and hungry people or food, children, sick people, someone who looks lonely, or other people suffering.

Development:

1. Have items to be bought arranged on the table.

2. Give each member five pennies with which to buy an item and allow them to "shop" for their item.

3. After the members have spent their money, show them some money and ask what are some things they can do with money.

4. Show them the piggy bank, bankbook, offering plate, movie ad, and food to help them think of some things to do with their money.

5. Ask, "What if we got paid and we spent all our money on candy? What would happen?"

6. Say, "God wants us to be responsible people and manage our money and our time well. He expects us to give part of our money and our time to the church."

7. Add, "You managed your time well this morning because you came to church."

8. Say, "There is a word that describes managing our money and our time well. It is called STEWARDSHIP." Write it on the board or chart tablet.

9. Then say, "Let's hear what Jesus said about someone who shared her money." Tell the story in your own words. Finish by having a member read the scripture.

10. Say, "During the worship service there is a time when we give our money to the church. We saw it in the Order of Worship bulletin when we studied about WORSHIP." Show the bulletin.

11. Ask, "When we give this money, what is it called?" See if they can tell you. "Our OFFERING." Write OFFERING on the board or chart tablet.

12. Ask, "What are some things that our offering can help our church do?"

13. Say, "Let's look at these pictures and see if they help us to think of some things."

14. Show pictures one at a time and discuss what our money does (for example: pastor—pays his salary; hungry people—provides food; children—provides classes for them; sick people—helps them to feel better).

15. Say, "When we go to the worship service, there will be a time when we are asked to give an OFFERING. We will give each of you the five pennies you were given when you came to class. When the OFFERING is taken you can put the pennies in the plate."

16. If time permits, you may want to arrange the chairs in small rows and practice passing the offering plate.

17. If your church has a special time for stewardship emphasis, you may wish to have special pledge cards for your class that emphasize giving time and talents as well as money (they will usually not have much money). The cards could have a place for pledging to pray, sing praises, attend church, read the Bible, and so on.

   Help them fill out their cards and allow them to come forward and place their pledges on your worship table. Then have a prayer of dedication, thanking God for the money and the time we have to share with others.

LESSON 8: FOOD CHEST/FOOD PANTRY

Definitions:

FOOD CHEST—The container in the foyer of the church (or wherever your church collects food) where members of the church place items of food

FOOD PANTRY—Where the food is taken to be given to people who do not have enough food to eat.
(If your church does not have this program, perhaps your class could be instrumental in getting it started.)

Bible Story:

Matthew 25:31–40. "The Least of These"

Scripture:

1 John 3:17

Preparation:

1. Call members or write to them suggesting that they bring canned food for the FOOD PANTRY this Sunday. You might have extra cans of food in case someone forgets to bring one. In the case of group homes or state school members, you may want to check with the responsible person as to whether it is possible for their clients to bring canned food. If not, provide the cans of food so that everyone has something to give.

2. Gather pictures of needy people—hungry, homeless, storm victims, for example.

3. Arrange a display of food (e.g., a piece of fruit, a vegetable, some bread, on a tray)

Development:

1. Show your class the tray of food.

2. Ask, "Have you ever been hungry?"

3. Ask, "What did you do about it?" (They might want to talk about favorite foods.)

4. Ask, "Did someone help you to get food? Who? How did the person know you were hungry?"

5. Ask, "What do you see in these pictures?" Hold the pictures one at a time so that everyone has a chance to see each picture. Discuss what is in the picture.

6. Help them to see that the people need to eat and have no food, or perhaps have no homes. Talk about the reasons they may be having these problems.

   - No job
   - No family
   - No friends
   - No church
   You may want to write these reasons on the board.

7. Ask, "What can we do to help people like these in the pictures?" Write any suggestions on the board.

8. Say, "Let's see what the Bible says about people like these."
   Read or tell "The Least of These," Matthew 25:31–40. Have a class member read or find the scripture.

9. Ask, "Did you bring a can of food with you today?"

10. Say, "When we go into the sanctuary for the worship service, we will take these cans of food and place them in the FOOD CHEST. These will go to the FOOD PANTRY for people like the ones in our pictures."

11. Ask, "Are you thankful you have enough to eat and a place to stay?"

12. Say, "Let's join hands and say a prayer for people who are hungry or those with no homes."

13. Sing "Our Father" ("Music for Church Words" section, page 89).

14. Make sure you allow some extra time for everyone to take their food to the FOOD CHEST, even if they are not staying for the worship service.

LESSON 9: PRAYER

Definition:

Talking to God

Bible Story:

Luke 11:1–13; Matthew 7:7–11. "Teach Us to Pray"

Scripture:

Matthew 6:9–13, the Lord's Prayer

Preparation:

1. Have two telephones ready for role-play on Sunday.

2. Cut out pictures of friends having fun together.

3. Provide a basket and paper for prayer requests.

4. Write the Lord's Prayer, one line at a time, on sentence strips.

Development:

(Hearing classes begin with #1. For nonhearing classes, let them examine the phones and discuss the special phones that help them communicate. Then begin with #3.)

1. Have the telephones on the table when class members arrive.

2. After they have had a chance to look at the phones, say, "We are going to play a telephone game." Let one member be the caller and another member be the person called.

3. After several members have had a chance to participate, ask, "Do you like to talk on the phone?"

4. "Let's look at pictures of friends having fun together." Show the pictures one at a time. Talk about what friends do when they are together.

5. Write conclusions on the board. If "talk to one another" is not mentioned, be sure to include it in your list.

6. "Does it make you feel good when your friends talk to you?"

7. Say, "God is our friend. God likes us to talk to him. What do we call it when we talk to God?" (Prayer)

8. Write PRAYER on the chart tablet or board.

9. Tell the Bible story, "Teach Us to Pray."

10. Say, "The special prayer Jesus taught the disciples is in our worship service every Sunday. We all say it together. It is called the Lord's Prayer. Let's say it together now."

11. Say the prayer one line at a time using the sentence strips, and have the class repeat each line. Then, let them come forward one at a time and attach a line to the board as the prayer is repeated.

12. Sing "Our Father" ("Music for Church Words" section, page 89).

13. Ask, "What are some things you would like to pray about?" Have each member write a request on a paper to place in the prayer basket. (Most of your class members will need help with this activity.)

14. Say, "Let's join hands in a circle, read our requests, and say a prayer to God about all these things."

LESSON 10: THANKSGIVING/PRAISE

Definitions:

THANKSGIVING—A special holiday in November

PRAISE—Saying, "Thank you" and "We love you" to God

Bible Story:

Psalm 136:1–9, 25–26. David, the Shepherd Boy and a Psalm of Praise

Scripture:

Colossians 3:17

Preparation:

1. Cut out pictures of things that inspire thankfulness—food, scenery, clothing, medicine, helpers (doctors, nurses, teachers, clergy), holiday pictures (Thanksgiving), homes, for example.

2. Have the pictures spread out on the table when the class begins.

3. Make simple puppets for the story (David, sheep).

Development:

1. Use the puppets to talk about how David was a shepherd boy and took care of the sheep. As he watched the sheep he made up songs to thank God for the beautiful world and all the good things in it. Many of David's songs are in the book of Psalms in our Bible. Later we will be reading one of the praise songs from Psalms together.

2. Ask, "Are you thankful for anything today?"

3. Ask, "Do you know what it means to be thankful?"

4. Ask, "Do you ever say 'Thank you' to someone?"

5. Write "Thank You" on the chart tablet or board.

6. Say, "Today we are going to write a thank-you note to someone who has been kind to us. Will you help?" (If there are enough helpers, let each member "write" a thank-you note to a friend, or if resources are limited, let the class compose the note to a person they choose. After the note is written each class member will sign it.)

7. Say, "Look at the pictures on the table. Choose a picture of something that makes you feel thankful." Discuss each picture chosen and place it on the chart tablet with tape or Plas-ti-tak.

8. Ask, "Who gave us all these things?" (They may or may not respond that God did.)

9. Say, "God made our world and all the things we enjoy, and God gave us the ability to make things that other people can enjoy. So, when we feel thankful, who should we say 'Thank you' to? [God] This is what we mean when we say THANKSGIVING." Read the scripture.

10. Write THANKSGIVING on the chart or board.

11. Say, "When we think of all the things God has given us, we want to tell God we love him. This is called 'Praise.'" Write PRAISE on the chart.

12. Say, "I have some friends here today to help me read a Thanksgiving prayer from the book of Psalms in the Bible."

13. Use the puppets to read the litany (Psalm 136:1–9, 25–26).

14. Say, "Why don't we do a thank-you litany like the one we just read? Let's look at the pictures we chose to decide what words we can put in our litany."

15. Use, "We thank you, God," or "We praise you, O God," for the response part of the litany. Write the words on a chart tablet as they are said. When the chart list is finished, read the "For" line and let the class respond with the response line. Example:

    For friends who love us . . .
    We thank you, God.

16. Go through the litany twice. Before the second time, tell the class that this will be our closing prayer. They may want to join hands.

LESSON 11: ADVENT/CHRISTMAS

Definitions:
> ADVENT—The church season beginning four Sundays before Christmas. A time for preparing our hearts to accept the baby Jesus as God's gift to us all
>
> CHRISTMAS—When we celebrate Jesus' birth

Bible Story:
> Luke 1:26–38, 46–55

Scripture:
> Luke 1:46–47

Preparation:
1. Gather items that give a message, for instance, newspapers, letters, books, Bible, a church bulletin.
2. Bring figures of an angel and Mary. (These may be part of a crèche or puppets. Large puppets can be made with 36-inch dowel rods using Styrofoam heads, yarn hair, coat-hanger arms covered with felt, and fabric costumes.)
3. Have paper and pencils for class to write, and folders to keep writings in.

Development:
1. Have items on the table for everyone to examine.
2. After class members have had time to look at the items on their own, pick up each item and discuss what it is and what it does for us. (Each tells us something about what has happened or what will happen.)
3. Ask if they can think of other things that give us messages. (Maybe radio, telephone, TV)
4. Say, "I want to tell you a story about a message that was given to someone. This message was given to a girl named Mary (Show the Mary figure) and it was told to Mary by an angel named Gabriel." (Show the angel figure.)
5. Tell the story, Luke 1:26–38, 46–55.
6. Let the class take turns holding the figures and retelling the story if they will. If not, let them simply hold and then place the figures on the table.
7. Ask, "What do you think Mary thought about the news that she would be the mother of Jesus, the Son of God?" Let someone read the scripture.
8. Ask, "Do you think she had to do some things to get ready for the baby Jesus to come?"
9. Sing, "Born in the Night, Mary's Child" (*The Presbyterian Hymnal,* number 30).
10. Say, "Our word for today is ADVENT, and it means a time to get ready for the celebration of the baby Jesus' birthday. When do we celebrate Jesus' birthday?" (CHRISTMAS, December 25)

11. Say, "CHRISTMAS is our other word. What do you like best about CHRISTMAS?"

12. Ask, "How can we get ready to celebrate CHRISTMAS?" Try to get the class to think of learning the Christmas story, doing nice things for others, or praying for ourselves and others. Help each person to write these things on a sheet of paper. (They may want to tell you what to write. Many will not be able to write that well. Several helpers will be needed for this activity.) Put the papers in a folder to take home at a later time.

13. Talk to them about preparing a gift to share with the church. Perhaps they could do a Christmas card or a banner for the church. Pictures of the Christmas story could go on the card. They will be learning about the Christmas story each Sunday during Advent.

14. Say, "Let's join hands and say a prayer that God will help us to get ready to celebrate CHRISTMAS, the birthday of Jesus."

LESSON 12: BETHLEHEM

Definition:

> The city in Judea where Mary and Joseph had to go to be registered for the census and where Jesus was born

Bible Story:

> Luke 2:1–7

Scripture:

> Luke 2:7

Preparation:

1. Have maps and pictures of different types of transportation displayed on the table or on the wall. Travel posters would be good.

2. Have puppets available for Mary, Joseph, and the innkeepers.

3. Have a life-size manger with some hay in it. Try to find someone in your church who will make a simple manger for you. (You will need the manger and doll again for another lesson. Plan to keep them handy or bring them back.)

4. Have a doll available for baby Jesus.

5. Have pictures of the Christmas story available for the class to begin coloring. Pastel chalks work well for coloring and give them a chance to work with a new medium. Pictures may be taken from Christmas coloring books and enlarged if necessary to go on your Christmas card. (We were fortunate to have a member of our church who is an artist. She drew the Victorian pictures for our card.) This project will take several weeks. If possible, provide a separate picture for each student to color. These may be cut out after they are colored, sprayed with a photo fixative to stick them to the background, and placed on a colored background to make the card. When completed, the card can be given to the church during a worship service and displayed in a prominent place for your special Christmas service (ours is Christmas Eve).

Development:

1. Let class members look at the maps and pictures.

2. Talk about taking trips and the things that are necessary to do before going on a trip. (Travelers must decide the route or way they are going and the mode of transportation. They must pack their clothes and, if they are traveling at mealtime, they have to decide if they will take their food or stop along the way.)

3. Today our word is BETHLEHEM. Ask if class members know the word. Explain that it is the town where Mary and Joseph went and where Jesus was born.

4. Say, "Listen to a story from the Bible that tells about the trip Mary and Joseph took. Let's see if they traveled the same way we travel."

5. Tell the story from Luke 2:1–7 in the Bible or use the puppets to tell the story.

6. Talk about what happened in the story. Why were they traveling, what did they take with them, and what happened when they got there?

7. Let class members play the story with the puppets, ending at the manger with the baby Jesus.

8. Sing, "Good Christian Friends, Rejoice" (*The Presbyterian Hymnal,* number 28, verse 1) and/or "O Little Town of Bethlehem" (found in most church hymnals or Christmas songbooks; for example, see *The Presbyterian Hymnal,* numbers 43 and 44).

9. Have a class member read or find the scripture, Luke 2:7.

10. Let class members take turns holding the baby Jesus.

11. Say, "Last week we talked about Advent. We said it was a time of preparing our hearts for the birth of the baby Jesus. One of the things we decided was to do something nice for someone else. We decided to make a Christmas card for the church, and we are going to start that project today."

12. Tell them they will be coloring pictures to go on the Christmas card. Say, "We have to be very careful as we color so that our Christmas card will be a special gift—our gift of love to the other members of the church." Give them some time to work on the project.

13. Have a prayer of thanks for the birth of Jesus.

14. Sing, "Silent Night" as a closing hymn (found in most church hymnals or Christmas songbooks; for example, see *The Presbyterian Hymnal,* number 60).

LESSON 13: SHEPHERDS

Definition:

The men who were watching the sheep when the angels told them that Jesus, the Savior, had been born

Bible Story:

Luke 2:1–20

Scripture:

Luke 2:20

Preparation:

1. Have a crèche available for Sunday.

2. Have a shepherd's staff available and a sheep (cardboard variety is fine).

3. Have colored pastel chalk and Christmas pictures available for the class to complete coloring if possible. Make arrangements to present the Christmas card during the church service next Sunday.

Development:

1. Show the class the staff and the sheep and ask if anyone knows what these items have to do with each other.

2. Someone may remember that the shepherd used the staff to help him care for the sheep. If not, explain how the sheep had to be watched at night because there were no fences and the wild animals would attack the sheep if the shepherds did not protect them.

3. Our word for today is SHEPHERDS. Write the word on the board or chart tablet.

4. Have the crèche displayed without the figures. Say, "Let's see what happened to the SHEPHERDS in our story today." Tell the Christmas story from Luke 2:1–20. As the story is told, place the characters around the stable.

5. Ask if they would like to tell the story and place the characters in the crèche. Explain that crèche is what we call the model of the Christmas story, the manger scene.

6. Help them remember the story by giving a character to each student, and as the story progresses helping them to place the character in the crèche.

7. After the characters are placed, read the scripture, Luke 2:20.

8. Finish coloring the pictures for the Christmas card. Tell them that next Sunday we will finish the Christmas card and present it to the church in the worship service.

9. Say a prayer of thanks that God sent the baby Jesus to show us God's love and help us to have new life.

10. Sing "Go Tell It on the Mountain" (*The Presbyterian Hymnal,* number 29) and "Silent Night" (found in most church hymnals or Christmas songbooks; for example, see *The Presbyterian Hymnal,* number 60).

LESSON 14: MANGER

Note: This lesson should occur the Sunday before Christmas.

If Christmas Eve or Christmas Day falls on Sunday, you may wish to consider not having the class that day. Many of the group-home and state-school residents will be visiting their families that day. It would be good to check with each group home and private home to see who will be able to come if the class is held.

Definition:

The animal feeding trough that became a bed for Jesus when he was born in the stable in Bethlehem

Bible Story:

Luke 2:1–20

Scripture:

Luke 2:7

Preparation:

1. Locate a pop-up storybook of the birth of Jesus.

2. Have puppets ready to let class members tell the story.

3. Find a manger and some hay for display, or if one is not available, use pictures of a manger. (You might be able to use the same manger as you did in the BETHLEHEM lesson on page 45.)

4. Bring a doll wrapped tightly in a blanket.

5. Have the special colored paper available so that the Christmas story pictures may be placed to finish the Christmas card for the church.

Development:

1. Have a manger on display when the class arrives.

2. Ask if anyone knows what this manger is for.

3. If hay is available, put some hay in the manger and explain that the animals ate their hay from the manger.

4. Put the word MANGER on the board.

5. Ask the class if they remember a Bible story that has a manger in it.

6. Tell them the Christmas story, using the pop-up book.

7. Ask, "In the story where was the MANGER and how was it used?" Read the scripture, Luke 2:7.

8. Show them the baby and let them take turns holding the baby.

9. Ask if someone would like to put the baby in our manger.

10. Ask, "In our story who was the baby in the manger?"

11. Sing, "Away in a Manger" (found in most church hymnals or Christmas songbooks; for example, see *The Presbyterian Hymnal,* numbers 24 and 25).

12. Ask if they would like to hear the story again and use the puppets.

13. Give a puppet to those who would like to participate. Tell the story, and as the characters are mentioned have them stand and hold their puppet or, if they are ready, have them hold the puppets and tell the story with the puppets.

14. Join hands and say a prayer.

15. Complete the Christmas card by laying the cutout pictures face down on newspaper, spraying with photo fixative and placing them on the card. The layout of the card should have been decided before this activity so that class members may be directed where their picture should be placed.

16. Decide which class members will help to present the card to the church.

LESSON 15: EPIPHANY

Note: This lesson should occur the Sunday following Christmas.

Definition:

A church celebration on January 6 remembering the visit of the Magi to the Christ-child

Bible Story:

Matthew 2:1–12

Scripture:

Matthew 2:11

Preparation:

1. Wrap a Christmas gift for each class member. These may be very simple or may be more elaborate. Suggestions: fruit, small pictures, bookmarks. They do not all have to be the same.

2. Have materials available for each member to make a gift for someone. Perhaps a bookmark, a paperweight, or a wall hanging. Or, if the alternate activity is used, have small cakes shaped like stars available. (Molds are available at kitchen shops.) Provide icing and decorations for the cakes. Have plastic wrap to wrap them to take home as a gift for someone, or place all the cakes on a tray to share with church members before the service.

3. Have Magi puppets and baby Jesus puppets available.

Development:

1. Have their gifts arranged on the table when class members gather.

2. Ask, "What are these? Did any of you receive gifts from someone this week?"

3. Discuss the gifts they received and let them talk about Christmas and how they celebrated.

4. Say, "We have celebrated ADVENT and CHRISTMAS and today we are getting ready for another celebration called EPIPHANY."

5. Write EPIPHANY on the board or chart tablet.

6. Say, "Epiphany is a time when we remember that baby Jesus received gifts from some very special travelers."

7. Tell the story of the visit of the Magi.

8. Ask if the class would like to do the story with puppets. Let them take turns holding the Magi puppets as the story is told again. If one of the class members is able to tell the story, allow that person to do it.

9. Say, "We are going to make a gift for someone today. You may give your gift to anyone you like."
   Suggestions: have 4" x 4" tiles and stickers that they may stick on them. Glue pieces of felt on the bottom so that they are smooth.

   Make bookmarks out of 2- or 3-inch ribbons. Let individuals put stickers on the ribbons.

   Or, as an alternate activity, use cakes to decorate and take home as a gift or to share with church members before the service.

10. Give each class member one of the wrapped gifts from the table. Tell them that this is their gift today to help them remember the time when the Magi brought gifts to the baby Jesus. Read the scripture Matthew 2:11.

11. Sing, "We Three Kings" (found in most church hymnals or Christmas songbooks; for example, see *The Presbyterian Hymnal,* number 66).

12. Join hands and say a prayer of thanks for all the gifts we have and especially the gift of God's son, Jesus.

LESSON 16: NURSERY

Definition:

A special room in the church where babies stay while their parents go to church school and to church

Bible Story:

Matthew 19:13–15; Mark 10:13–16. Jesus and the Children

Scripture:

Mathew 18:5

Preparation:

1. Gather some baby items for display.

2. Ask someone who has a baby in the church to bring the baby to class for a short visit.

3. Prepare a "Concentration" game, using no more than ten numbers. Gather pictures of babies or baby items. (You will need five different pictures, two of each one.) Put the numbers 1 to 10 on pieces of construction paper. Tape on a poster board at the top of each so that the construction paper may be lifted to reveal pictures underneath.

4. Check with someone in your church nursery to make sure that it is convenient for the class to come to see them on Sunday.

Development:

1. Have baby items displayed when class members arrive or, if a baby is present, let them look at the baby and talk to it. (You may need to explain that they may not hold the baby if the mother does not want them to do so.)

2. Allow time for them to look at the items. Talk about babies.

3. Show some pictures of babies.

4. Play "Concentration." Concentration is a matching game. Five sets of pictures are used. Pictures are placed beneath each number. As two numbers are called the pictures are revealed. When a player matches two pictures it is a "win." When there is a match the pictures are removed. (The player gets to hold them.) Play until all are matched. If class members are enjoying the game and there is enough time, put the pictures under different numbers and play again.

5. Ask if they remember when they were babies or when someone in their family was a baby.

6. Tell them that Jesus loved the babies and small children. Say, "There is a story in the Bible that tells how Jesus loved the children." Tell "Jesus and the Children."

7. Say, "Our church loves babies. We have a special room where babies can stay on Sunday morning while their parents attend church. Does anyone know what that room is called?"

8. Say, "It is the NURSERY." Write NURSERY on the chart tablet or board.

9. Ask, "Does anyone know where the NURSERY is in our church?"

10. Say, "We are going to leave class a little early today and go by the NURSERY in our church."

11. Then say, "Let's join hands and thank God for the babies and their parents in our church."

12. Sing, "Jesus Loves the Little Children" (*The Celebration Hymnal,* number 447).

LESSONS 17–18: BIBLE

Definition:

A collection of writings that we believe contain the story of God and how God relates to men and women. Also called the Word of God, or the scriptures

Bible Story:

2 Kings 22–23; 2 Chronicles 34; Deuteronomy 6:4–5, 28:1–14. The Lost Scroll

Scripture:

2 Timothy 3:16

Preparation:

1. Have Bibles available for everyone.

2. Prepare a scroll to show them. Use two dowel rods. Glue or staple each end of a rectangular paper to a dowel rod. Write the scripture verse on the scroll. Roll up from both ends to form the scroll. Tie with a ribbon.

3. Rent or purchase a video about the Bible. A suggestion is *The Amazing Book,* distributed by Multnomah.

4. Reserve a TV and VCR for viewing the video.

Development:

1. Say, "Today we are going to talk about the BIBLE."

2. Write BIBLE on your board or chart tablet.

3. Ask, "What is the Bible?"

4. Give time for the class's responses.

5. Say, "We are going to see a video about the Bible. Let's look at this together and see if we can learn something about the Bible."

6. Show the video.

7. Give everyone a Bible.

8. Tell them the Bible is God's word to us, the story of what God is like and of God's love for us.

9. Say, "The Bible has two main parts." Write "The ____ Testament" and "The ____ Testament" on the board and see if they can remember the words to fill in the blanks. (Old; New)

10. Let them look at their Bibles. Show them the Old and New Testaments. Show them how to find Psalms in the middle of the Bible. Talk about the stories that are found in each section of the Bible. Talk about the different kinds of books there are—history, poetry, prophets, Gospels, letters. Show them the chapters and verses.

11. Tell the story of "The Lost Scroll," 2 Chronicles 34

12. Show them the scroll. Say, "There is a verse from the Bible that has been written on this scroll." Ask a class member to come forward and unroll the scroll so that the verse may be read.

13. Sing "The Bible" ("Music for Church Words" section, page 88).

14. Have a closing prayer and thank God for giving us the Bible to guide and help us each day.

Note: There is more content in this lesson than can be handled in one session. Break the lesson where it is necessary to do so. Begin the second session with a review of the first.

If the video is interesting to the class show it a second time or let them practice finding books, chapters, and verses in their Bibles. They will need individual help with this activity. Your class might enjoy making a scripture scroll to take home with them.

LESSON 19: CHRISTIAN

Definition:

A person who believes in and tries to follow Jesus

Bible Story:

Acts 11:19–30. The Church at Antioch

Scripture:

Acts 11:25–26

Preparation:

1. Cut out pictures that represent groups of people such as:

men	firefighters
women	police
farmers	doctors
athletes	anything else you want to depict

2. Write the above words on pieces of colored paper.

Development:

1. Have the pictures on the table when the class arrives.

2. Put the colored papers with the words representing groups of people on the board or on a poster. Let class members decide what group (or groups) each picture represents and help them place that picture under the appropriate word.

3. Ask if they can think of other groups not represented in your pictures.

4. Say, "There is another word we need to explore today. That word is CHRISTIAN."

5. Write CHRISTIAN on the board or chart tablet.

6. Ask, "Have you ever heard someone say, 'I am a Christian,' or 'He or she is a Christian'? Do you know what it means?"

7. Say, "There is a story in the Bible that tells how this word first came to be used." Tell the story from Acts 11:19–30.

8. Ask, "What were some of the things the people at Antioch were doing that made other people call them Christians? Were they good things to do?" (They believed in Christ, cared about others, told others about Jesus.)

9. Ask, "What are some things we do that would make others call us Christian" (You may have to help them get started with this.) Write their suggestions on the board.

10. Let them write some of these ideas on a paper with the word "CHRISTIAN" at the top. These may be placed in notebooks to be taken home later. (Helpers will be needed to assist in this project. Those who have difficulty writing can sometimes connect the dots to make a word like CHRISTIAN.)

11. Join hands and sing "Lord, I Want to Be a Christian" (*The Presbyterian Hymnal*, number 372).

12. End with a prayer.

LESSON 20: CROSS

Definition:

A symbol of the sacrifice of Jesus Christ, when he gave his life for each of us that we might live in fellowship with God

Bible Story:

Matthew 27:1–2, 11–56

Scripture:

John 3:16

Preparation:

1. Have boards prepared to build a cross for the classroom. The wood should be notched to fit together. Class members will take turns nailing the pieces together. Or: Have small wooden crosses notched to fit together. Class members may glue the pieces together. Each class member would have a cross to take home.

2. Bring artificial flowers to decorate the cross if you build the large cross.

3. Provide a cross or a picture of a cross to show the class.

Development:

1. Show a cross or a picture of a cross to the class.

2. Write CROSS on the board or chart tablet.

3. Ask, "When you see this cross, what does it mean to you?"

4. Write their responses on the board or chart tablet.

5. Say, "I want to tell you a story about this cross." Tell the story in your own words, taken from Matthew 27:1–2, 11–56.

6. Say, "Since Jesus was crucified on a cross, every time we look at a cross it reminds us of what Jesus did for us and of how much God loves us."

7. Read (or have one of your reading students read) John 3:16. It is helpful to highlight the verse and use a bookmark to find the page. A nonreading student can then find it.

8. Ask, "Did Jesus die on the cross? Did he stay dead?" Tell them that there is a verse in the Bible that says Jesus is risen. Let a class member help find the verse (Mark 16:5–6), which you have marked, perhaps in another Bible.

9. Say, "He came back to life and is with us today. We can talk to him anytime we want."

10. Ask, "Would you like to make a cross for our classroom as a symbol to remind us that God loves us?"

11. Let class members take turns nailing the cross together, or all put their individual crosses together.

12. If a large cross was used, give each member a flower. Say, "Each person in our room has a flower. We will come forward one person at a time and put our flowers on our cross. The flowers will be a symbol to us of the life that Jesus gave to each of us by his death on the cross." (If you made the smaller crosses, you may still wish to have a large cross to decorate, or you may decorate the picture that you brought.)

13. If the small crosses were used, tell the class that they may take their own home with them to remind them of God's love for us and the life Jesus gave us by dying on the cross.

14. Sing "The Old Rugged Cross" (*The Celebration Hymnal,* number 327) or "When I Survey the Wondrous Cross" (*The Presbyterian Hymnal,* number 101).

15. Join hands and say a closing prayer thanking God for the gift of life Jesus gave to us.

LESSON 21: BAPTISM

Definition:

A ceremony in the Christian church in which the pastor places water on the head or lowers the person into the water. This is a symbol of God's gift of new life to us and of our willingness to follow Jesus. Babies are baptized, showing God's gift of life to them and the church's commitment to teach them to follow Jesus. One must be baptized to become a member of the church.

Bible Story:

Matthew 3:13–17. The Baptism of Jesus

Scripture:

Matthew 28:19–20

Preparation:

1. Prepare a series of flash cards with symbols on one side and the words they stand for on the other side. Examples:

2. Ask the pastor to come and talk to the class about baptism.

3. If the baptismal font is movable, you may want to have it in the class, or you may want to take the class into the sanctuary early so that they may see the font before the service. Be sure to make arrangements if you plan to go into the sanctuary early.

4. Prepare a poster card with the word BAPTISM on it.

Development:

1. Have the flash cards on the table when the class arrives.

2. Say, "What is a symbol?" Give them a chance to respond.

3. Say, "A symbol is a picture of something that reminds us of a word or words we understand." Gather the flash cards with symbols and show them one at a time, allowing the class members to tell what the symbol means. (Keep these cards to use again in later sessions. You may wish to laminate the cards to make them more durable.)

4. Say, "Symbols help us to see what a word or thought looks like."

5. Say, "Today our word is BAPTISM." Show them the word.

6. Say, "When a person is baptized in our church, the pastor places water from a bowl we call the baptismal font on that person's head."

7. Ask, "Have any of you been baptized? Have any of you seen someone being baptized?"

8. Say, "Sometimes we are baptized when we are babies and we don't remember what it was like. Other people have to tell us about it. Have you seen babies being baptized during our worship service?"

9. Say, "The pastor of our church, [name], is here with us today. He/she is going to tell us about our word BAPTISM."

10. Depending on what the pastor says, you may want to tie it together by saying something like this: "Baptism is like a symbol. When we are baptized in our church, it reminds us of God's gift of life to us and of our pledge to follow the teachings of Jesus. When a baby is baptized in our church, it shows God's gift of life to them and the church's pledge to teach them to follow Jesus."

11. Tell the class the story of "The Baptism of Jesus," from Matthew 3:13–17.

12. Let someone find the scripture that you have marked in your Bible, and then read Matthew 28:19–20 to the class.

13. Say, "Let's join hands and sing 'We Are Buried with Christ'" ("Music for Church Words" section, page 95).

14. Say a prayer and adjourn to the sanctuary to view the baptismal font if it could not be brought to your room.

LESSON 22: COMMUNION

Definition:

A special meal Jesus had with his disciples to remind them of his gift of life to them. He asked that all believers have this meal together often, to remind them of his love. The meal is composed of grape juice or wine and bread or a cracker, to remind us of Jesus' body and his blood, or his life that was given for us.

Bible Story:

Matthew 26:17–30; Mark 14:12–26; Luke 22:7–23; John 13

Scripture:

1 Corinthians 11:23–25

Preparation:

1. Gather a sample of the service and elements for Communion in your church. Have these visible on a table when class members arrive.

2. Find a teaching picture of the Last Supper and have it ready to show the class. (Your children's classes should have one of these to loan you.)

3. Gather some robes or stoles with sashes to use as costumes for picture posing.

4. Have ready the flash cards of symbols from the session on BAPTISM (see #11 in "Development").

Development:

1. Allow class members to touch the service and samples of the elements you have displayed.

2. Ask, "Has anyone seen these things before?"

3. Ask, "What is it called when we use these things in our church service?"

4. Write the word COMMUNION on the chalkboard or chart tablet.

5. Define COMMUNION.

6. Say, "I want to tell you a story about the first communion."

7. Say, "Jesus and the disciples were in Jerusalem. It was time for the celebration of Passover. Passover is the celebration of the time when God saved the Israelites from dying when they were in Egypt. Jewish people still celebrate Passover every year so that they can remember God's care for them."

8. Continue with the story of the Lord's Supper in your own words.

9. Show a picture of the Last Supper.

10. Let the class take turns posing the picture. You may have simple robes or stoles with waist ties that will serve as costumes.

11. Show the flashcards of symbols. Say, "Remember these symbols help us to think of other things such as

Love   Handicapped   Ladies

Men   No Parking   No Smoking

12. "And what are the symbols of Communion?" (Bread; Wine or Cup)

13. Let the class draw a picture of the symbols of Communion to place in their folders. (Some of your members will need help doing this activity. A teacher might draw the symbols with dots and let the member connect the dots.)

14. Read 1 Corinthians 11:23–25.

15. Join hands for closing prayer and sing "In Remembrance" ("Music for Church Words" section, page 90).

Note: If it is convenient to do so and the members are baptized, you may wish to ask for permission to actually have Communion in your classroom. Your pastor would need to be present to do this. *Or:* You may wish to teach this lesson on a Sunday when Communion is being served in the church.

Sometimes baptism information is difficult to obtain. If it is unknown and the member wishes to receive communion, you might want to consult with your pastor.

LESSON 23: LENT

Definition:

The church season that begins with Ash Wednesday and continues until Easter. It is a time for Christians to take a look at their lives and see if they are living as God wants them to and to make the corrections that are needed.

Bible Story:

John 15:1–12

Scripture:

John 15:12

Preparation:

1. Provide two trees with branches—one that is bare and one that has leaves or blossoms.

2. Make blank cards shaped like apples for everyone, with hangers to hang on the tree with leaves. (Punch holes in the cards and use yarn for the hangers.)

3. Provide small papers where good deeds can be written and then pasted on the apple cards.

4. Provide glue or paste.

5. Have a large calendar showing Ash Wednesday and Easter.

Development:

1. Write LENT on a piece of poster board. Pass it around for the class members to see.

2. Say, "Today our word is LENT. Has anyone heard that word before?" (They may have heard "lint" in reference to fabric lint.)

3. Say, "Lent is the church season we are now celebrating. It is the time period between Ash Wednesday and Easter." Show them a large calendar.

4. Say, "It is a time when we each take a look at our life and see if we are being a good person and if we are doing what God wants us to do. It is a time when we tell God those things we may be doing that are wrong and ask God to forgive us."

5. Ask, "How do we know what God wants us to do?" (The Bible, teachers, pastors)

6. Ask, "What are some things you are doing that would please God?" (Make a list of those things on the board or chart tablet.)

7. Say, "Let's sing a song about the Bible, where we learn about good things to do." Sing "The Bible" ("Music for Church Words" section, page 88).

8. Ask, "What are some wrong things we would like to ask God to forgive?" (Make a list of those things on the board or chart tablet.)

9. Say, "Let's have a prayer and ask God to forgive all the wrong things we do."

10. Say, "I have a plant I want us to see this morning, and I want to tell you a story about what Jesus said about a plant."

11. Turn to John 15:1–12 and tell the story in your words. End by reading John 15:12.

12. Say, "You see that one of our trees has branches with leaves and one does not. Jesus said we are like this plant. We are like the branches. Jesus is like the vine or the trunk of the plant. If we (the branches) are not connected to Jesus (the vine) we cannot bear any fruit. The fruit is like the good things we do."

13. Say, "We want to be sure we have good fruit on our branches. What are some good things we do? Look at our list." Read the list on the board and help them to add to it.

14. Give each person the apple cutout and the "good deed" paper on which to write their good deed. Help them to write the good deed and paste the paper on their apple. (Let the class member do as much of this activity as possible.)

15. Let class members put their fruit on the good tree.

16. Say, "Remember that LENT is the time when we look at our lives and see if we are doing good deeds or bad deeds. We want to make sure our lives are connected to Jesus so that we can have good fruit on our tree."

17. Say, "Let's join hands around the tree and thank God for helping us to bear good fruit and ask God to forgive our mistakes."

LESSON 24: PALM SUNDAY

Definition:

The Sunday when we celebrate the triumphal entry of Jesus into Jerusalem, at the beginning of Holy Week

Bible Story:

Mark 11:1–10

Scripture:

Mark 11:9b

Preparation:

1. Bring leafy branches for dramatization.

2. Bring palm fronds to make crosses.

3. Provide glue.

4. Bring scarves for headdresses—strips of material to tie around the heads of the drama participants.

Development:

1. Say, "Have you ever been to a parade? What was it like?"

2. If the students are having trouble getting started, say, "People line up on both sides of the street and other people walk or ride by. The people cheer and celebrate." Give them time to discuss parades.

3. Say, "Our words for today are PALM SUNDAY." Write the words on the board or chart tablet. (Keep them for next Sunday).

4. Say, "We will celebrate Palm Sunday in our church next Sunday."

5. Say, "The Bible tells us about a time when there was a celebration and the people there had something like a parade."

6. Open the Bible to Mark 11:1–10 and tell the story in your own words, using the branches as a prop. Have a class member find and read the scripture.

7. Say, "The reason we will celebrate Palm Sunday next Sunday is to help us remember the time when Jesus rode into Jerusalem."

8. Ask, "Would you like to have a play about this story? We will need someone to be Jesus." Choose someone. "We need several disciples." Choose. "We need an owner for the donkey." Choose. "And the rest of us will be the people who are celebrating."

9. As they dramatize the story, remind them of the facts of the story.

10. Say, "Since next Sunday is Palm Sunday, I thought we might make something we can wear to the worship service the week after, on Easter Sunday."

11. If there is some group or class at the church that has done something nice for your class, you might suggest that the class make additional crosses to share with them.

12. Ask, "Do you remember what the CROSS means?" Show them a cross. If there is more than one, pass them around and let the class look at them.

13. Say, "The cross reminds us of what Jesus did for us. He died on the cross and came back to life so that all of us could live."

14. Say, "We are going to make crosses out of the palm fronds. Today we will glue them together and on Easter we will wear them to the worship service."

15. When they have finished the crosses, sing "Psalm 100" ("Music for Church Words" section, page 93).

16. Have a closing prayer.

LESSON 25: THE LAST SUPPER

Definition:

The Passover meal Jesus had with his disciples just before he was arrested and hung on the cross

Bible Story:

Luke 22:10–20

Scripture:

Mark 14:26

Preparation:

1. Provide a picture of the Last Supper.

2. Bring leafy branches.

3. If more crosses need to be made, provide palm fronds and glue.

4. Bring unleavened bread or matzo and grape juice and cups.

Development:

1. Ask, "What did we talk about last Sunday? Do you see the words on the board?"

2. Say, "PALM SUNDAY. We are celebrating Palm Sunday today."

3. Ask, "Who remembers something about the story of Palm Sunday? Who was there? What were they doing?" Continue to ask questions until they have reconstructed the story.

4. Pass out the leafy branches and say, "Let's sing a praise song and wave our branches."

5. Sing "Psalm 100" ("Music for Church Words" section, page 93).

6. Let the class finish the crosses if they have not.

7. If you are taking Easter crosses to another group, choose two or three people to take the crosses to them.

8. Say, "After Jesus came into Jerusalem, it was time for the celebration of Passover. Passover is the celebration of the time when God saved the children of Israel from their slavery in Egypt. Jewish people still celebrate Passover every year so that they can remember God's care for them."

9. Take your Bible and turn to Luke 22:10–20. Tell them the story of the Last Supper.

10. Show them the picture. Say, "People call this meal the Last Supper. We sometimes have a meal like this when we worship together. Does anyone remember the word for that meal?"

11. Say, "COMMUNION." Write it on the board. "We have Communion because Jesus asked us to do that to remember what he did for us when he died on the cross and came back to life so that we could live."

12. Say, "Let's look at the picture and we will pretend we are there with Jesus. They ate something called unleavened bread and we are going to taste some."

13. Pass the bread around so that they can taste it. Say, "Jesus told us that this bread is to remind us of his body, which he gave for us."

14. Let class members take turns posing the picture of the Last Supper as you tell the story. Give them the words to say and let them play the story. You might do this several times if more than one person is interested in playing Jesus and the disciples. Have the unleavened bread and the cups of juice to use in the story. End by reading the scripture, Mark 14:26.

15. Join hands and sing "In Remembrance" ("Music for Church Words" section, page 90).

16. Close with a prayer.

LESSON 26: RESURRECTION

Definition:

Coming back to life after having been dead. At Easter we celebrate Jesus' resurrection.

Bible Story:

John 19, John 20:1–18

Scripture:

John 11:25

Preparation:

1. Bring a cross, a picture of the crucifixion (or you might bring a small crucifix), and a picture of the women visiting the tomb.

2. Provide Styrofoam cups, soil, beans to plant, and spoons to scoop the soil.

3. Have a water pitcher available for watering the beans.

4. Bring pins or tape to put the palm crosses on each participant.

5. Write the word RESURRECTION on a card to be passed around.

Development:

1. Say, "Today is Easter!"

2. Ask, "What do we think about when we say the word 'Easter'?" List the class's answers on the board or chart tablet. They may respond with such things as Easter eggs, bunnies, candy, new clothes. Some may have a grasp of Jesus' resurrection. Discuss their answers.

3. Have a cross, a crucifix, or a teaching picture of the crucifixion and one of the empty tombs displayed.

4. Say, "Let's look in the Bible and see what happened on the first Easter Day." Begin the story with the arrest of Jesus, include the crucifixion, and end with the women going to the tomb and finding that Jesus had risen.

5. Pass the cross and the two pictures around for the class to see.

6. Ask, "When Jesus was crucified on the cross, how do you think his disciples felt?" Invite someone to come to the board and draw a sad face.

7. Ask, "How did they feel when they found that Jesus had come back to life?" Invite someone to draw a happy face.

8. Say, "Today we have a Church Word that means coming back to life after being dead. That word is RESURRECTION." Pass the word around the room so that everyone may see.

9. Say, "Because Jesus was crucified on the cross, was buried, and came back to life, we can all have life with him."

10. Read from John 11:25. "Jesus said to us, 'I am the resurrection and the life. Those who believe in Me shall live even if they die.'"

11. Sing "Jesus Christ Is Risen Today" (*The Presbyterian Hymnal,* number 123).

12. Say, "Each of us is going to plant a bean today to help us remember the resurrection. We will put the bean in some soil and water it. The bean will begin to die as the plant begins to live, and we will see a plant rise through the soil and come out where it can grow. When we look at our plants we will remember that Jesus gave us life."

13. Say, "Everyone needs to put his or her name on the Styrofoam cup before we put in the soil."

14. Say, "We will keep these beans in our classroom and water them until they begin to grow. Then you can take them home and maybe plant them outside."

15. Say, "Let's join hands and thank God for Jesus and his gift of life to us."

16. Finish by singing "I Believe" ("Music for Church Words" section, page 87).

LESSON 27: HOLY SPIRIT

Definition:

The third member of the Trinity. The comforter, helper, enabler Jesus sent to dwell within his followers after his ascension. Holy Spirit was sent to the disciples at the celebration of Pentecost (a Jewish celebration or festival).

Bible Story:

Acts 2:1–8, 12–39, The Gift of the Holy Spirit

Scripture:

John 3:16; Acts 2:1–4; John 14:26; Luke 4:18; Romans 14:17; Romans 15:13

Preparation:

1. Prepare for each person in the class a colored construction-paper heart with the word "love" written on it. Cut them into simple puzzles (two pieces for those who need it very simple and more pieces for those with more ability). Place the pieces in individual envelopes with the number of pieces written on them.

2. Prepare symbols for wind and fire.

3. Prepare cards for each word or expression describing Holy Spirit: comforter, teacher, helper, brings goodness, brings peace, brings joy, brings hope.

Development:

1. Light the candle and sing "Every Time I Feel the Spirit" (found in most church hymnals; for example, see *The Presbyterian Hymnal,* number 315).

2. Have a class member read John 3:16.

3. Give everyone a heart puzzle with the word "love" written on it. Allow time to put the puzzles together. Ask if anyone can tell what the puzzle is. Say, "The heart is a symbol for love. It makes us think of love, but it isn't love."

4. Talk about love.

    A. "Can you see love?"

    B. "Can you touch love?"

    C. "Can you describe love?"

5. Say, "Love is a feeling—something inside us. We can't see it but we can tell it is there by our thoughts and actions. We know it is a gift from God because the Bible tells us that 'God is love.'"

6. Say, "We want to talk about something else that is a gift from God. After Jesus went to heaven to be with God, the disciples were in Jerusalem for the Jewish festival called Pentecost. Jesus had promised before he left to send Holy Spirit to them as a comforter. Holy Spirit was to teach them the truth, stay with them, and live in them. This was the spirit of Jesus and God."

7. Say, "Let's read about what happened." Read from Acts 2:1–4 or tell the story in your own words, being sure to include the references to wind and fire. Use the symbols you made for wind and fire.

8. Say, "In this story there were two symbols we often use to identify Holy Spirit. Can you guess what they were?" (Wind and fire)

9. Put the wind and fire symbols next to the love symbol on the board and say, "Just like love, we can't see Holy Spirit but we know Holy Spirit is there by our actions and thoughts."

10. Say, "There are Bible verses that describe what Holy Spirit is like." Write HOLY SPIRIT on the board.

11. Say, "Let's read some of the verses." Have class members listen as the scripture passages are read and tell you the descriptive words. Have the words from the version you have read written on colored paper. Get class members to put them on the board under HOLY SPIRIT.

    John 14:26   (comforter, teacher, helper—helps us remember what Jesus said)

    Luke 4:18   (helper—helps us do God's work)

    Romans 14:17 (brings goodness, peace, joy)

    Romans 15:13 (brings hope)

12. Sing "Spirit" (*The Presbyterian Hymnal,* number 319). Or: sing "Every Time I Feel the Spirit" (found in most church hymnals; for example, see *The Presbyterian Hymnal,* number 315).

13. Have a prayer time.

14. Extinguish the candle.

LESSONS 28–29: CREED

Definition:

A statement of what we believe

Scripture:

Matthew 16:13–18

Preparation:

Bring a collection of objects such as replicas of animals, a basket, a candle, a flower.

Development:

1. Display the objects on the table. Allow students to look, touch, and handle the objects.

2. Pick the objects up one at a time and ask if anyone can describe them.

3. Have one of the teachers stand in front of the class and ask the members to describe that person. Write their responses on the board.

4. Say, "We have been describing with words what we are seeing."

5. Say, "Our word today is CREED. A creed is a statement of what we believe or what we think is most important."

6. Say, "Every Sunday we stand during worship and say what we believe about God and about Jesus and about Holy Spirit."

7. Ask, "Do you remember how the Creed that we use in worship begins?" ("I believe [or "We believe"] in God the Father Almighty . . .")

8. Ask, "Would you like to write your own Joy Class creed? We can do it together."

9. Say, "Let's begin with what we believe about Jesus." Write "Jesus" on the board or chart tablet.

10. Ask, "What is something you know or believe about Jesus?" Give members a chance to think of things they have learned about Jesus. They may require some prompting and discussion to think of something.

11. Write the class suggestions on the board or chart tablet.

12. Follow the same procedure using the word "God."

13. Follow the same procedure using the words Holy Spirit.

14. If more items are needed and time is available, go through the same procedure with "Church."

15. When the lists are completed put the results in a creed form beginning with "I believe," for example, "I believe that Jesus is the Son of God."

16. Have class members stand and repeat each line as you say it.

17. Sing "I Believe" ("Music for Church Words" section, page 87).

18. Have a closing prayer.

Note: This lesson covers a large amount of material for one lesson. It can easily be extended to two sessions. The second session activity might involve decorating a poster board on which to place the finished creed. You might use stencils of a cross. Each class member would be given a stencil, a sheet of paper, and acrylic chalk or crayons. When the crosses are colored, students may cut around them and glue them on the poster board to make a border. The creed should be copied on a white paper and glued to the center of the poster board. This can be displayed in the classroom and used as part of your opening worship time for subsequent sessions.

You may want to talk to your pastor and see if the creed could be used in a worship service. Your class could present the creed to the congregation and then it could be used in worship that Sunday.

LESSON 30: CHURCH MEMBERSHIP

Definition:

A belonging that people are given when they have presented themselves to the church and have declared that they are followers of Jesus by being baptized

Bible Story:

Romans 12:4–15. One Body, Many Members

Scripture:

Matthew 28:18–20; Matthew 18:19–20

Preparation:

1. Gather pictures of groups of people. Save these pictures for use with SESSION/ELDER.

2. Prepare a sentence strip with the words CHURCH MEMBERSHIP written on it.

3. Invite your pastor to visit with your class regarding church membership and arrange your schedule to fit the pastor's schedule.

4. Prepare simple cutouts of a church silhouette on white paper with doors that have been cut to open. Provide colored paper to glue the church cutout on, leaving the doors free to open. Each class member will be asked to write his or her name inside the church door.

Development:

1. Have pictures of groups of people on the table in front of class members.

Girl and boy scouts	School class
Choir	Dance class
Swim team	Football team

   Let each class member choose a picture and talk about that group—who they are, what they do, and so on.

2. Ask, "Have you ever belonged to a club or a group of some kind?" Give time for discussion.

3. Say, "Today I would like to talk to you about another kind of membership or belonging—CHURCH MEMBERSHIP." Write the word on the board or prepare a sentence strip with the words and pass it around the group.

4. Ask, "What is the church?" Give them some time to respond. They may respond with:

   A. A place to worship God

   B. Where I see my friends

   C. A place to learn about God

   D. A building

   Remind them of the word CHRISTIAN and ask if anyone remembers the meaning. (One who believes in and follows Jesus)

5. Say, "In the Bible, Paul tells us what the church should be like." Hold the Bible open to Romans 12:4–15 as you tell them the following paraphrased version: "He said: We have many different parts to our bodies (heads, hands, feet, eyes, mouths, to name a few), and each part does a special thing for us. (Talk about what we do with hands, feet, and so on.)

   "The church is like that too. There are many people, but all are connected to Jesus. Each person has special gifts or abilities that can be used to help the other people in our church. Some people are preachers, some are teachers, some can give more money than others, some can cheerfully forgive others, some can show great love, and some can pray.

   "Paul also said: The church members should rejoice in hope, keep trying when they have trouble, pray, help those who need help, be happy with those who are happy, cry with those who are sad, and never feel that they are better than anyone else."

6. If the pastor has come to visit today, this may be a good time for some pastoral comments regarding church membership for the class members or, if time is not an issue, you may wish to wait until the next activity is completed.

7. Hand out the church cutouts with the colored paper and glue sticks. Help class members glue their church to the colored paper, being careful not to glue the doors shut. Ask them to open the doors and write their names inside the church. Some may need help writing their name.

8. Tell the class that you would like them to think about becoming members of the church. Say, "If you have never been baptized you would need to be baptized in order to join the church. If you have already been baptized, you can join the church by telling the pastor and the session that you love Jesus and want to follow his teachings." (You may wish to have your pastor take over this portion of the lesson, or if you feel your class is not ready for this step, you may wish to omit this. If your church baptizes infants, there may be some of your class members with extreme disabilities who have never been baptized and could be baptized as adults—or as children, if this is the case. Discuss this with your pastor. It will be necessary to talk with each group home representative and obtain permission before proceeding with church membership. They are generally cooperative, but may not have information regarding baptism.)

9. "Do any of you feel that you would like to become a member of this church?" Arrange to speak with these people privately and with the pastor. Make all the arrangements necessary with their guardians or responsible caregivers.

10. Sing "Blest Be the Tie That Binds" (*The Presbyterian Hymnal,* number 438).

LESSON 31: SESSION/ELDER

Note: These terms may be altered to fit the governing body of your denomination.

Definitions:

SESSION—The group of elders currently conducting the business of the church and leading in its work

ELDER—A member of the church who has been elected by the congregation and ordained to conduct the business of the church and lead in the work of the church. Once elected and ordained to the position of elder, the member remains an elder whether or not the member is currently serving on the session.

Scripture:

1 Timothy 5:17

Preparation:

1. Ask two or three elders who are currently serving on the session to come to the class. Ask them to be prepared to tell the class about one thing they do at session meeting.

2. Gather pictures of groups of people meeting together; for example, in the church, boy or girl scouts, Congress, school, football huddle.

Development:

1. Ask, "Who has played Simon Says?" Listen for the class's responses and let them share their experiences.

2. Say, "If we were playing Simon Says, the first thing we would need to have is a leader. Who will be our leader?"

3. Ask, "If our leader says, 'Clap your hands,' would we clap our hands? [No] If our leader says, 'Simon says, clap your hands,' would we do it? [Yes]"

4. Allow the "leader" to give two or three commands and then choose several other leaders if there are volunteers.

5. Say, "We have been a group of players and [insert the names of the leaders] have been our leaders."

6. Say, "Let's look at some pictures of some other kinds of groups and see if they have leaders."

7. Show the class the pictures one at a time and encourage discussion by asking questions about the pictures.

8. Put the pictures on the board or chart tablet and write the name of each group beside them.

9. Say, "There is a group of people in our church called the session." Write SESSION on the chart tablet or board.

10. Say, "The session takes care of the business of the church and leads in the work of the church. What is the work of the church?" See if the class can answer. If not, give some suggestions or show some pictures to help them think—teaching, worshiping, helping others to know about Jesus.

11. Say, "People who are members of the session are called elders." Write ELDER on the board. "Say, 'ELDER.'"

12. Say, "Elders are elected by the people in the church. Some elders are serving on the session and some are not."

13. Ask, "Have you ever met an elder?"

14. If some of your teachers are elders, identify them as such.

15. Say, "Today we have some people in our class who are elders in our church. They are serving on the session."

16. Introduce the elders, and have each elder tell something they do at session meetings.

17. Say, "We have a Bible verse that tells us something about elders." Let a student help find the verse. (1 Timothy 5:17)

18. Read the verse and say, "Let's all join hands and say a prayer to thank God for giving us elders and the session to take care of our church."

Note: You may need to rearrange this session to accommodate the schedules of guest elders.

LESSONS 32–33: DEACON

Definition:

A person who is elected and ordained by the church to take care of the sick, sad, bereaved, or hungry members of the congregation as well as to share in the happiness of the members of the congregation

Bible Story:

Luke 10:30–37, The Good Samaritan

Scripture:

Acts 6:1–6

Preparation:

1. Invite a deacon and/or a telecare person (a volunteer who phones church members to see if they have special needs or concerns) to visit the class.

2. Gather pictures of people who are sick, sad, or hungry, and pictures of people who are getting married or having birthdays or other celebrations.

3. Provide costumes or puppets to play the story.

4. Prepare a happy face and a sad face on separate pieces of paper.

Development:

1. Have the pictures of people who are troubled or happy on the table when the class members arrive.

2. Show the pictures one at a time and let the class decide if the people are happy or sad. Hold up the happy or sad face or let a class member do so. See if they can tell you what is happening to the people.

3. Ask them, "Have you ever been sad? happy?" Allow time for discussion.

4. Ask, "Did you have someone to talk to about your sadness or happiness? Did that make it better?"

5. Say, "We like to share things that happen to us with someone who loves us, don't we?"

6. Let someone find the scripture, Acts 6:1–6, and say, "The Bible tells us about a time when some church members decided that they needed some special people to help take care of the people in their church who were hungry and sad."

7. Say, "The people who were chosen were called deacons." Write DEACON on the board or chart tablet.

8. Say, "We have deacons in our church. Some of them are visiting us today." Introduce the visiting deacons.

9. Say, "They are here to tell you what they do to help us."

10. Have the deacons tell the class members what they do.

11. Say, "A deacon serves the people in the church when they need help or comfort. Who would like to pretend to be a deacon and serve the class members?" Let two or three members take turns serving cups of water to the others.

12. Say, "There is a Bible story that tells us about taking care of someone who is hurt and in trouble. Would you like to hear it?"

13. Tell the story "The Good Samaritan," Luke 10:30–37.

14. Ask what happened to the man who was traveling.

15. Ask, "Who helped him?"

16. Ask, "Would you like to do this story using the puppets?"

17. If time permits, let them do the story now. If not, say, "Next Sunday we will do the puppet show. Be sure that you are here to help."

18. Say, "Let's join hands and say a thank-you prayer to God for giving us deacons in our church to help us."

Note: If the puppet show is saved for next Sunday, begin by reviewing the Bible story and talking about the people who were in the story. Allow several sets of players to do the story.

Let them make a list of things they can do to be helpful to others. These may be put in their notebooks to take home later. Sing several songs.

LESSON 34: PASS THE PEACE

Definition:

What we do at the time in the worship service when we shake hands with each other or hug each other and say, "The peace of the Lord be with you" and the other person responds with, "And also with you"

Bible Story:

John 14

Scripture:

John 14:27

Preparation:

1. Bring pictures of places people might greet one another. (Church, school, front door, store)

2. Prepare one or two cards with PASS THE PEACE written on them.

Development:

1. Ask, "What are some words or actions we use when we first see each other?" (Suggestions could be: Hi, Hello, How are you? Howdy; shake hands, wave, sign hello, peace, or shalom from a book on signing.)

2. Write these on the board or chart tablet.

3. Say, "These are called greetings."

4. Show pictures of different places where we use greetings. Ask, "Where are some places we use greetings?"

5. Sing a greeting song: Use the music to the round "Are You Sleeping" [or Frère Jacques] and use the words,

    Hello, ____. Hello, ____.
    How are you? How are you?
    We are glad to see you. We are glad to see you.
    At our church. At our church.

6. Let the students take turns going to someone and shaking hands while singing the song.

7. In your own words, tell the story that is in John 14. Say, "Before Jesus was crucified on the cross, he told his disciples that he would be going to be with the Heavenly Father. He told them that he was the Son of God, and that when he left them Holy Spirit would come to be with them and to help them know the right way to live. Then he talked to them about peace."

8. Read John 14:27.

9. Say, "There is a time in our worship service when we PASS THE PEACE. This is our word for today. Does anyone know what we mean when we say PASS THE PEACE in our worship service?" Show them the card with the words written on it.

10. Say, "We go to someone at the service and say, 'The peace of the Lord be with you,' and the other person answers, 'And also with you.'" (See if they can tell you what words are used before you tell them.)

11. Ask, "What does peace mean? Does it mean calm, friendliness, rest?"

12. Say, "Let's practice so that we can do it during the worship service today. We need two people."

13. Let them take turns passing the peace to one another.

14. Join hands and sing "I've Got Peace like a River" (*The Presbyterian Hymnal,* number 368).

15. Say a prayer of thanks to God for all God's promises.

PART 3
MUSIC FOR
CHURCH WORDS

I Believe

Kinley Lange

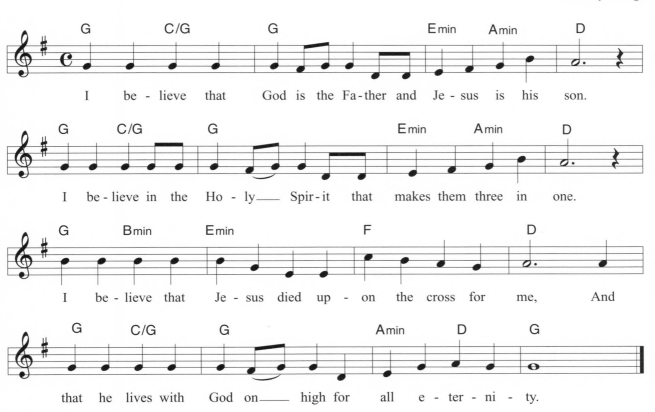

The Bible

Kinley Lange

The Bi - ble is the Word of God and what it says is true. It tells us what is right and wrong; it speaks to me and you. It tells us of the an - cient days, of peo - ple long a - go; Of how their lives are just like ours and how God loves us so.

Our Father

Kinley Lange

In Remembrance

Kinley Lange

As of - ten as you eat this bread, as of - ten as you drink this cup,

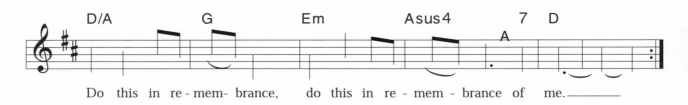

Do this in re - mem- brance, do this in re - mem - brance of me.

I Was Glad

Kinley Lange

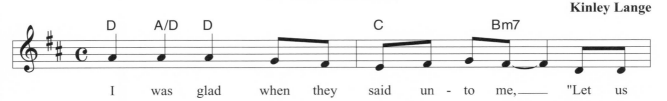

I was glad when they said un-to me,_____ "Let us

go in-to the house of the Lord."_____ I was glad when they

said un-to me,_ "Let us go in-to the house of the Lord,_____ and we'll

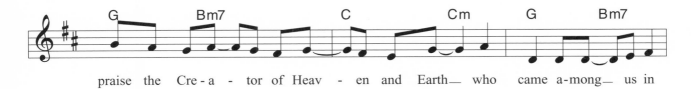

praise the Cre-a - tor of Heav - en and Earth_ who came a-mong_ us in

hum - ble birth."_____ I was glad when they said un-to me,_ "Let us

go in-to the house of the Lord."_____ I was glad when they

said un-to me,_____ "Let us go in-to the house of the Lord."

Our Pastor

Kinley Lange

*Substitute name(s) and pronoun (him, her, them)

© *Copyright 1997 Kinley Lange. Used by permission.*

Psalm 100

Kinley Lange

Make a joy - ful noise un - to—— the Lord,—— all——

peo - ple make a joy - ful noise.—— Make a joy - ful noise un -

to—— the Lord,—— all—— peo - ple make a joy - ful noise.——

Serve the Lord with—— glad - ness, come in - to God's pres - ence with a

song. Serve the Lord with—— glad - ness, come in - to God's presence with a

song. Make a peo - ple make a joy - ful—— noise.

The Peace

Kinley Lange

The peace of our Lord be with you; and al - so with you.

We Are Buried with Christ

Kinley Lange

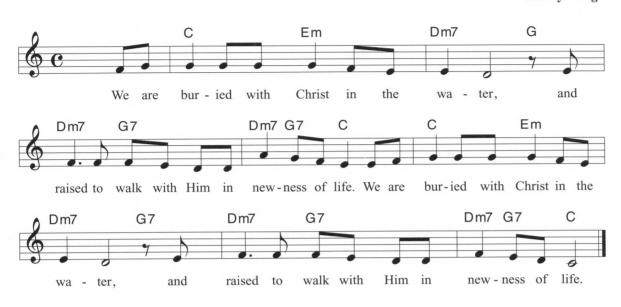

APPENDIX

LETTER TO PARENTS OF
PROSPECTIVE CLASS MEMBERS

(This letter was sent to the parents of members of a social group called the Stars announcing the beginning of Joy Class.)

(today's date)

Dear Stars' Parent:

At various times I have visited with some of you regarding a church school class for our "special" adults. My husband and I, like many of you with your children, have reached a point where Tim no longer has a class that fits his needs at our church. Therefore, we decided to begin a new class at (name of church).

The literature for the class is entitled *Feed All My Sheep* by Doris C. Clark and is distributed by Geneva Press. The class format is a discussion type to provide another "safe" place for our adults to interact with one another and with the class leaders. I feel there is a need for our adults to have someone besides a parent or house parent with whom to discuss problems and joys. We have two teams of leaders, who are enthusiastic, responsible individuals with much to offer our adults.

If you already have a church school class that is meeting your needs—Hooray! If not, please consider visiting ours.

We will begin on (date) at (time) and will continue each Sunday morning at the same time. There will be coffee, fruit or fruit juice, and muffins for a time of fellowship as the class begins. Church services are at (time) and (time), and class members are encouraged to participate in the full program of the church.

(Name of church) is located at (address of church). If you have questions or comments, call (name of class coordinator) at (phone number with area code).

Sincerely,

(name of class coordinator)
Coordinator

SOLICITATION LETTER SENT TO GROUP HOMES

(This letter was sent to a list of group homes provided by the Mental Health and Mental Retardation office.)

(today's date)

Dear Group Home Manager:

We are writing to invite your group-home residents to a new class that is beginning at (name of church). The class is designed for adults over twenty-one years of age who have developmental disabilities.

The literature for the class is entitled *Feed All My Sheep* by Doris C. Clark and is distributed by Geneva Press. The class format is a discussion-interaction type, to provide another "safe" place for adults to express themselves and share problems or joys with their friends and class leaders. Our class leaders are enthusiastic, energetic, and responsible individuals with much to offer our adults.

The class will begin on (date) at (time) and will continue each Sunday morning at the same time. There will be coffee, fruit or fruit juice, and muffins for a time of fellowship as the class begins. Church services are at (time) and (time), and class members are encouraged to participate in the full program of the church.

(Name of church) is located at (address of church). Please feel free to call (name of class coordinator) at (phone number with area code) if you have questions regarding this program.

Sincerely,

(name of class coordinator)
Coordinator

JOY CLASS REGISTRATION

Name: _____   Birthday: _____

Address: _____   Baptism: Yes   No   (Circle one)

_____   Date of Baptism _____

Phone: _____

Allergies or Food Restrictions:

_____

_____

Physical or Emotional Problems We May Need to Know:

_____

_____

Medications:

_____

_____

In Case of Emergency, Please Call:

_____

_____

Please mail or bring to (church name), Joy Class, (church address).

SOLICITATION LETTER FOR JOY CLASS BUDDIES PLACED IN THE BULLETIN ON SUNDAY

JOY CLASS NEEDS YOU !!!!!!!!

We are organizing a group of people to be Joy Class Buddies. This group is for those members of the congregation who would like to support Joy Class (our class for adults with developmental disabilities) but do not want to teach on a regular basis. Buddies might be used to provide refreshments, provide transportation, help with special class projects, or just be a friend and sit with a Joy Class member during worship.

Requirements for service:

The ability to share your love

An occasional meeting (probably not more than two a year)

A willingness to visit Joy Class once in a while to get to know our members. (Those providing refreshments are encouraged to do this, but it is not necessary.)

If you would like to learn more about being a Joy Class Buddy, please fill out this form and place it in the offering plate.

Name: _____

Address: _____

_____

Phone: _____

THANK-YOU POEM FOR CHURCH BULLETIN

You invited us into your church

with a welcome smile and acceptance.

You have given us a place to gather,

and teachers to help us to learn

about Jesus and God and worship;

but most important of all,

you have given yourselves.

For it is only through you

that we are able to see God's love.

THANK YOU!

THE MEMBERS OF JOY CLASS

SUGGESTED
RESOURCES

RELIGIOUS EDUCATION RESOURCES

Augsburg Fortress Publishing House. *I Live in God's Grace*. A Bible-based course designed for people with mild to moderate disabilities. Includes several sessions focusing on the betrayal, crucifixion, and resurrection of Jesus. Participant Book—#TK15-62525; Leader Guide—#TK15-62526. Augsburg Fortress Publishing House, 426 S. Fifth Street, Box 1209, Minneapolis, MN 55440-1209. Phone: 1-800-328-4648.

Augsburg Fortress Publishing House. *I Live in God's Love*. A Bible-based course for adults with mild to moderate disabilities. Worksheets, stories, flash cards, and discussion explore topics relating to the participants' lives in family, work, and social situations. Participant Book—#15-62317; Leader Guide—#15-62318. Augsburg Fortress Publishing House, 426 S. Fifth Street, Box 1209, Minneapolis, MN 55440-1209. Phone: 1-800-328-4648.

Augsburg Fortress Publishing House. *I Live in God's Promises*. A Bible-based course designed for people with mild to moderate disabilities. Participant materials include fourteen two-page, full-color leaflets, as well as activity cards. Leader's guide has activity ideas and session plans classified as easy, middle, or difficult. Participant Book—#15-62523; Leader Guide—#15-62524. Augsburg Fortress Publishing House, 426 S. Fifth Street, Box 1209, Minneapolis, MN 55440-1209. Phone: 1-800-328-4648.

Baptist Sunday School Board. *Special Education Teaching Packet*. Includes a resource kit containing teaching pictures and Bible-learning activities—#076737111; a teacher guide for teaching adults, youth, or children with developmental disabilities, containing Bible background, teacher development helps, and step-by-step instructions for leading the sessions—#0767365755; a Bible study in the form of a participant's study help containing Bible story, memory verses, learning activities, suggestions, and questions—#0767365771. Lifeway Christian Resources, Publisher, Customer Service Center, 127 Ninth Ave. N, Nashville, TN 37234. Phone: 1-800-458-2772.

Bethesda Lutheran Homes and Services, Inc. *Special Religious Education Resource Manual*. Contains information about books, curriculum, music, and organizations relating to religious education for people with disabilities. Bethesda Lutheran Homes and Services, Inc., 700 Hoffmann Drive, Watertown, WI 53094-6294. Phone: 1-800-369-4636, ext. 418.

Building Community Supports Project. *Dimensions of Faith and Congregational Ministries with Persons with Developmental Disabilities and Their Families*. A bibliography and address listing of resources for clergy, laypersons, families, and service providers. Building Community Supports Project, American Association on Mental Retardation, Bill Gaventa, 31 Alexander St., Princeton, NJ 08540.

Christian Reformed Church Publications. *The Friendship Series*. A three-year curriculum for youth and adults. Units deal with "God, Our Father," "Jesus, Our Savior," and "Jesus' Spirit, Our Helper." Heavy emphasis on biblical content interpreted somewhat literally. Includes Group leader's kit, teacher's manuals, and student resource packets. Christian Reformed Church Publications, 2850 Kalamazoo Avenue SE, Grand Rapids, MI 49560. Phone: 1-800-333-8300.

Cokesbury. *Bridges: A Curriculum for Persons with Disabilities—13 Lessons*. Cokesbury, 201 Eighth Ave., P.O. Box 801, Nashville, TN 37202, Phone: 1-800-672-1789.

Cokesbury. *Living in Faith: A Resource for Teachers of Older Youth and Young Adults Who Are Retarded* (1986). Fifty-two sessions dealing with various aspects of faith and faith involvement as well as physical development and sex education. The sessions are designed for use with mildly disabled individuals. Units are not particularly connected and could be used independently. Good teacher resource. Cokesbury, P.O. Box 801, Nashville, TN 37202. Phone: 1-800-672-1789.

National Council of Churches. *Expanding Worlds: Christian Education Resources for Adults Who Are Retarded* (1976). Lesson plans and other resources. National Council of Churches, Room 706, 475 Riverside Drive, New York, NY 10115. A limited quantity is available through the National Council of Churches. May be borrowed from the National Christian Resource Center, (1-800-369-INFO, ext. 284) for thirty days for the cost of return postage.

Stewart, Sonja M., and Jerome W. Berryman. *Young Children and Worship*. Designed for children without disabilities but is adaptable for adults. Utilizes class participation and visual presentation. Westminster/John Knox Press, 100 Witherspoon Street, Louisville, KY 40202-1396. (Information on workshops may be obtained by writing Dr. Stewart at Western Theological Seminary, Holland, MI 49423, or Mr. Berryman at Christ Church Cathedral, 1117 Texas Avenue, Houston, TX 77002.)

Stewart, Sonja M. *Following Jesus: More about Young Children and Worship*. Designed for children without disabilities but is adaptable for adults. Utilizes class participation and visual presentation. Westminster John Knox Press, 100 Witherspoon Street, Louisville, KY 40202-1396. (Information on workshops may be obtained by writing Dr. Stewart at Western Theological Seminary, Holland, MI 49423.) To be published in Spring 2000,

MUSIC RESOURCES

Morstad, David. *Music in Special Religious Education*. Bethesda Lutheran Homes and Services, 700 Hoffmann Drive, Watertown, WI 53094. Phone: 1-800-369-INFO.

Pinson, Joe. *All God's People Love to Sing*. A collection of forty-five songs. Joe Pinson, P. O. Box 491, Denton, TX 76202. Phone: 940-382-4379.

Westminster/John Knox Press. *The Presbyterian Hymnal*. Westminster John Knox Press, 100 Witherspoon St., Louisville, KY 40202. Phone: 1-800-227-2872.

Wilson, Etta, ed. *My Play a Tune Book: Twelve Favorite Bible Songs*. JTG of Nashville, 1501 County Hospital Rd., Nashville, TN 37218. Distributed by Ingram Book Co. Phone: 1-800-937-8000.

Word Music/Integrity Music. *The Celebration Hymnal* (1997). Word Entertainment, 3319 West End, Suite 201, Nashville, TN 37203-6890. Phone: 1-888-325-9673.

NEWSLETTERS

A.M.E.N.(" . . . all may enter" news). Presbyterians for Disabilities Concerns, Room 5627, Attn: Lew Merrick, 100 Witherspoon Street, Louisville, KY 40202-1396.

Breakthrough. Quarterly publication containing curriculum, information, and music. Bethesda Lutheran Homes and Services, Inc., A. L. Napolitano, Executive Director, 700 Hoffmann Drive, Watertown, WI 53094-6294. Phone: 1-800-369-4636, ext. 418.

Networks: For Those Ministering within the Disabilities Community. A quarterly publication in cooperation with The Special Gathering, Inc., Christian Council on Persons with Disabilities, 7120 West Dove Court, Milwaukee, WI 53223.

Presbyterians for Disability Concerns Newsletter. Available with membership in PDC, it contains ministry models, resources, and news about what congregations are doing. PDC is a network of the Presbyterian Health, Education, and Welfare Association (PHEWA). Membership information may be obtained by writing PHEWA, 100 Witherspoon Street, Room 3041, Louisville, KY 40202-1396.

The Chapel Carillon. Three publications per year, includes information regarding ministry to persons with disabilities and music by Joe Pinson. Dennis D. Schurter, Director, Denton State School, Chaplaincy Department, P.O. Box 368, Denton, TX 76202-0368. Phone: 940-891-0342.

OTHER RESOURCE BOOKS

Costello, Elaine. *Religious Signing: The New Comprehensive Guide for All Faiths.* Illustrated by Lois Lehman, with more than five hundred signs, prayers, and blessings. Bantam Books, Inc., Publisher, 666 5th Avenue, New York, NY 10103. Phone: 212-765-3535.

Costello, Elaine. *Signing: How to Speak with Your Hands.* Illustrated by Lois A. Lehman (1983). Bantam Books, Inc., Publisher, 666 5th Avenue, New York, NY 10103. Phone: 212-765-3535.

Lukens, Betty. Various sets of characters and objects with a printed teacher's manual, memory verses, scripture references, additional helps, an alphabetical index, and a numerical index of all pieces. Call for a catalog. Betty Lukens, Inc., P.O. Box 1007, Rohnert Park, CA 94927. Phone: 1-800-541-9279.

Okhuijsen, Gijs, and Cees van Opseeland. *In Heaven There Are No Thunderstorms: Celebrating the Liturgy with Developmentally Disabled People* (1992). The Liturgical Press, St. John's Abbey, Collegeville, MN 56321. Phone: 320-363-2213.

Riekehof, Lottie L. *The Joy of Signing: The Illustrated Guide for Mastering Sign Language and the Manual Alphabet.* Gospel Publishing House, 1445 N. Boonville Ave, Springfield, MO 65802. Phone: 417–862–2781.

VIDEOTAPES

Amazing Book. Multnomah Publishers, Inc., 305 W. Adams St., Sisters, OR 97759. Distributed by Spring Arbor Distributors. Phone: 1-800-395-5599.

Information videos on aspects of developmental disability are available from Bethesda Lutheran Homes and Services, 700 Hoffmann Dr., Watertown, WI 53094. Phone: 1-800-369-4636, ext. 418.